THE GREAT
PYRAMID:
A Miracle In Stone

THE GREAT
PYRAMID:
A Miracle In Stone

by Joseph A. Seiss, D.D.

(Originally published in Philadelphia, 1877)

New Introduction by Paul M. Allen

1817

HARPER & ROW, PUBLISHERS, San Francisco
Cambridge, Hagerstown, Philadelphia, New York,
London, Mexico City, São Paulo, Sydney

Library of Congress Cataloging in Publication Data

Seiss, Joseph Augustus, 1823-1904.
    The Great Pyramid.

    Reprint of the 1877 ed. published by Porter & Coates, Philadelphia, under title: A miracle in stone.
    Includes bibliographical references.
    1. Giza. Great Pyramid of Cheops.   I. Title.
[DT63.S46 1981]   932   80-19801
ISBN 0-06-067211-0

81 82 83 84 85   10 9 8 7 6 5 4 3 2 1

INTRODUCTION

On a beautiful spring morning some months ago, my son and I joined an enormously long cue stretching for several blocks in Great Russell Street, London, waiting to enter the gates of the British Museum to see what has become without doubt one of the most popular exhibitions ever shown there. Nearly a million people, far exceeding the most sanguine hopes of the sponsors — the London Times and the Trustees of the British Museum — have stood for as many as four solid hours (as did we) to visit the extraordinary "Treasures of Tutankhamen Exhibition," a choice selection of objects from the richest archeological find of this century, transported from the Cairo Museum to London for the first time.

As we viewed the remarkable exhibition, my thought reverted to Cairo and its Museum where decades before I had studied these same objects, along with many others on display there. In addition, I vividly recalled the trip out of the city to the desert plain where for the first time in this life I had the unforgettable experience of standing before what is unquestionably the very greatest of *all* wonders remaining to us from ancient Egypt — the Great Pyramid itself.

It has been said — and rightly, I believe — that only when one actually stands at the base of the Great Pyramid of Gizeh (also known as the Pyramid of Cheops) does the stupendous nature of the structure become apparent.

On the basis of sheer size alone, the Great Pyramid is certainly one of the most impressive buildings in the world. Its ground area includes some thirteen acres, which is almost three times the space enclosed by the walls of the Vatican at Rome. Its summit towers some one hundred fifty feet higher than the top of Sir Christopher Wren's dome crowning St. Paul's Cathedral, London.

Nevertheless, statistics of this sort — and there is an abundance of them — by no means convey the wonder of this mighty architectural achievement. Only when the Great Pyramid is seen in its relation to the expanses of the starry heavens and as the expression of the working of earthly, geometric principles can one begin to glimpse something of the secret wisdom of the ancient Mysteries embodied in its construction.

Today when an almost irresistible force attracts men to the cultural-spiritual life of ancient Egypt — as evidenced by the extraordinary attendance at the British Museum, the public interest shown in contemporary efforts to preserve various Egyptian monuments (those at Abu Simbel, among others) in face of the rising level of the Nile, and a widespread preoccupation with books on Egyptian culture, mythology, magic, esotericism, art and religious customs — the Great Pyramid, "the House of God," as it was called in ancient times, is also attracting much attention.

Before the Great Pyramid one instinctively pauses in quiet amazement, awed in the presence of this great creation, this mighty legacy from the ancient world and its Mysteries. It stands silent witness to the almost unbelievable skill of its builders, whose technical knowledge of heavenly and earthly dynamics clearly transcended in many respects that of even our most modern technology.

On the other hand, the individual human being finds an especially intimate, personal relationship to the Great Pyramid when he reflects that in it are expressed not only laws of the vast cosmos, but also proportions derived from *the human body itself*. In reality, since man as the microcosm is a replica of the macrocosm, these two elements are one and the same. As Rudolf Steiner once observed, "In the Great Pyramid everything — length, breadth, depth, the architectural forms, the interior, to the last detail — was modelled on the measures, the proportions of the heavens which at the same time are those of the human body, for they are identical."

This very unusual book now lying before the reader is certain to enhance his interest in the cultural-spiritual life of ancient Egypt. In a remarkably fresh, living way Joseph Seiss has drawn upon an abundance of sources to bring forward a wealth of fascinating, lucid evidence that the Great Pyramid of Gizeh is indeed *the* central expression of the Mystery Wisdom, the esoteric secrets of ancient Egypt, making this extraordinary structure a veritable "Miracle in Stone."

— Paul M. Allen

Botton Hall,
Danby/Whitby
Yorkshire, England.
March, 1973.

PREFACE.

THIS book is meant to give a succinct comprehensive account of the oldest and greatest existing monument of intellectual man, particularly of the recent discoveries and claims with regard to it.

If the half that learned and scientific investigators allege respecting the Great Pyramid of Gizeh be true, it is one of the most interesting objects on earth, and ought to command universal attention. It has been unhesitatingly pronounced, and perhaps it is, "the most important discovery made in our day and generation."

Simply as an architectural achievement, this mysterious pillar, from the time of Alexander the Great, has held its place at the head of the list of "The Seven Wonders of the World." But, under the researches and studies of mathematicians, astronomers, Egyptologists, and divines, it has of late been made to assume a character vastly more remarkable. Facts and coincidences so numerous and extraordinary have been evolved, that some of the most sober and philosophic minds have been startled by them. It would verily seem as if it were about to prove itself a sort of key to the universe—a symbol of the profoundest truths of science, of religion, and of all the past and future history of man. So at least many competent persons have been led to regard it, after the most thorough sifting which the appliances of modern science and intelligence have been able to give it.

Particularly in Scotland, England, and France has the subject elicited much earnest interest. Quite a number of works and treatises, most of them voluminous, costly, and learned, have been devoted to it, and not without a marked and serious impression. St. John Vincent Day, Fellow of the Royal Scottish Society of Arts, member of sundry institutions of Engineers, and honorable librarian of the Philosophical Society of Glasgow, says :

"A former published work on the subject, besides one or two papers in the transactions of a scientific Society, have of necessity brought me into contact with every shade of opinion as to the various theories respecting the Pyramid, and the facts belonging to it. I have thus been enabled, both by verbal and written discussions and arguments, to ascertain the weight of evidence on which theories, assertions, contradictions, and alleged facts have been supported ; and I can only state that in those cases where the Pyramid subject has been examined into with a diligent spirit of inquiry, that is with the aim of not merely strengthening preconceived notions or prejudices, but to evolve absolute realities, I have not yet met any one but who is more or less convinced by the modern theory."— Preface to *Papers on the Great Pyramid*, 1870.

In this country, the publications on the subject have been very circumscribed. A few tracts, short papers, review articles, or incidental discussions in connection with other subjects, is about all that has thus far appeared from the American press. And as the European books are mostly large, expensive, and not readily accessible, comparatively few among us have had the opportunity of learning what has developed in this interesting field. A just résumé of the matter, of moderate length and price, in plain and easy form, would seem to be needed and specially in place.

In the absence of anything of the sort, and with a view to what might in measure supply the want, the preparation of the following Lectures was undertaken. How far the effort has succeeded, the candid reader will determine. It has at least been honest. Persuaded of the varied worth of the subject, the author has endeavored to be accurate in his presentations, and as thorough as the space would allow. For his data concerning the Pyramid he has been obliged to rely on the original works of explorers, to which due reference is given. Though in Egypt in the latter part of 1864, with a view to some personal examinations, a severe sickness, contracted in Syria and Palestine, prevented him from accomplishing the purpose for which he visited the land of the Pharaohs. But his interest did not therefore abate. In 1869 he gave out a small publication on the Great Pyramid, and having tried to master and digest what has thus far been adduced by others, he now ventures a larger exhibition of the case as it presents itself to him. The intricacies of mathematics and astronomy, so deeply involved in these pyramid investigations, he has intentionally avoided, seeking rather to explain for the many than to demonstrate for the few. He has confined himself mostly to descriptions and statements of results, which he has sought to give in a way which all readers of average intelligence can readily follow and understand.

If what he has thus produced is so far favored as to promote a more general and deeper inquiry and study into this surprising and most perfect monument of primeval man, the chief object of the author will have been attained. The interest awakened by the Lectures at their oral delivery during the past winter, and the numerous applications to procure them in print, also encourage the belief that, with the notes and amplifications since added, they may perchance be acceptable and serve a good purpose. With the hope, therefore, of thus contributing something towards the furtherance of correct science, true philosophy, and a proper Christianity, the author herewith commits these sheets to the press, and to an appreciative and indulgent public.

PHILADELPHIA, JUNE 25th, 1877.

CONTENTS.

LECTURE FIRST.

GENERAL FACTS AND SCIENTIFIC FEATURES.

LECTURE SECOND.

MODERN DISCOVERIES AND BIBLICAL CONNECTIONS.

(7)

LECTURE THIRD.

ANALYSIS OF TRADITIONS, OPINIONS, AND RESULTS.

APPENDIX.

EXTRACTS FROM RECENT WRITERS.

"EVERY student who enters upon a scientific pursuit, especially if at a somewhat advanced period of life, will find not only that he has much to learn, but much also to unlearn. As a first preparation, therefore, for the course he is about to commence, he must loosen his hold on all crude and hastily adopted notions, and must strengthen himself, by something of an effort and a resolve, for the unprejudiced admission of any conclusion which shall appear to be supported by careful observation and logical argument, even should it prove of a nature adverse to notions he may have previously formed for himself, or taken up, without examination, on the credit of others. Such an effort is, in fact, a commencement of that intellectual discipline which forms one of the most important ends of all science."—
Sir John Herschel.

"THE fair question is, does the newly proposed view remove more difficulties, require fewer assumptions, and present more consistency with observed facts, than that which it seeks to supersede? If so, the philosopher will adopt it, and the world will follow the philosopher."—*Grove's Address to the British Association for the Advancement of Science.*

(9)

IS. XIX. 19.20.— AN ALTAR TO יהוה IN THE MIDST OF EGYPT.

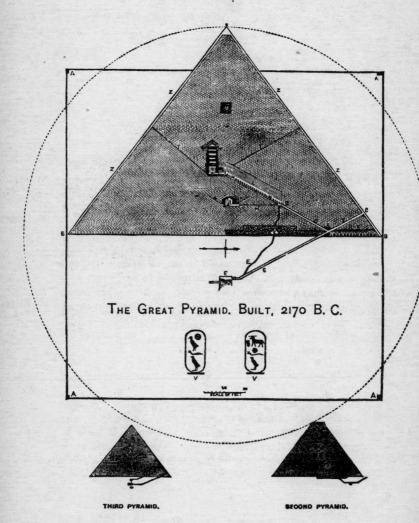

THE GREAT PYRAMID. BUILT, 2170 B. C.

THIRD PYRAMID.

SECOND PYRAMID.

INDICATIONS ON THE DIAGRAM.

A, A, A, A, Corner sockets of the Pyramid's base.

B, B, B, Pyramid cut in half, viewed from the east.

C, C, C, Entrance passage.

D, D, First ascending passage.

E, E, E, The well.

F, The subterranean chamber.

G, G, G, Native rock, left standing.

H, Horizontal passage to Queen's Chamber.

I, Sabbatic or Queen's Chamber.

J, Grand niche in Queen's Chamber.

K, K, Ventilating tubes to Queen's Chamber.

L, Grand Gallery.

M, M, M, Rampstones, incisions, and vertical settings along the sides of Grand Gallery's base.

N, Great step at south end of Grand Gallery.

O, Granite leaf in anteroom to King's Chamber.

P, P, Anteroom to King's Chamber.

Q, King's Chamber.

R. Grand Coffer in King's Chamber.

S, S, S, S, S, Chambers of construction.

T, T, Ventilating tubes to King's Chamber.

U, Supposed undiscovered Chamber.

V, V, V, Cartouches of the two Kings, Shufu and Nem-Shufu, otherwise called Cheops or Suphis, and Sen-Suphis or Noh-Suphis, under whose co-regency the Great Pyramid was built.

W, W, Sections of next two pyramids, showing their interior openings.

X, X, Al Mamoun's forced passage.

Y, Time-marks of the building of the pyramid.

Z, Z, Z, Z, Casing-stones, now gone.

☞ The shading in crossed lines indicates what parts of the Pyramid are red granite; the other portions, as far as known, are of limestone, of a color approaching yellowish-white.

☞ By the use of a magnifier the lettering and indications on the diagram will be brought out in ample distinctness, where not sufficiently clear to the naked eye. The print is reduced photographically from a drawing of large size.

(11)

As wards, who long suppose
    All that they spend to be
    Their guardian's liberality,
Not what inheritance bestows,
Their thanks to others ignorantly pay
        For that which they
    At last perceive to be their own,
To their rich ancestors obliged alone ;—
    So we vainly thought
        Ourselves to Greece much bound
        For arts which we have found
    To be from higher ages brought,
By their as well as our forefathers taught.

                        Gale's " Court of the Gentiles."

A MIRACLE IN STONE:

OR,

THE GREAT PYRAMID OF EGYPT.

Lecture First.

GENERAL FACTS AND SCIENTIFIC FEATURES.

ONE of the ablest of England's Egyptological writers has said that Egypt is the anomaly of the earth's present surface. The very adaptations and adjustments of the air and solar distances, by which vegetable life is sustained in other countries, here give place to another code, framed expressly for the Nile. The same may be said of it with regard to its place in history. It has always been somewhat aside from the general current of affairs, having its own unique constitution and life, and yet closely related to all civilized humanity. Through whatever path, sacred or profane, we propose to go back to the beginnings, Egypt is never entirely out of view. Closely secluded from all the rest of the world—the Japan of the ages—it still lies at the gateway of the traditions of Judea, Greece and Rome; intermingles with all the Divine administrations, and connects, in one way or another, with some of the most famous names and events in the annals of time.

It is a land which has been reclaimed and created by the Nile, that "High Priest of streams,"

> Whose waves have cast
> More riches round them, as the current rolled
> Through many climes its solitary flood,
> Than if they surged with gold.

The shoreline, around the several mouths of this mysterious river, describes a large semicircle, to which the emptying streams run out like the ribs of a spread fan, or like so many spokes of a wheel. The centre of this arc is the first rocky elevation on the south, about ten miles west of Cairo. And, strange to say, that centre is artificially and indelibly marked by a massive stone structure, of almost solid cyclopean masonry, of a form found in no other country, and at once the largest and oldest building now standing on the face of the earth. This hoary monumental pile is *The Great Pyramid of Gizeh*, of which it is my purpose to present some account.

THE CHART.

In order to aid the mind by means of the eye, I have caused a diagram of the Great Pyramid to be prepared, which, if first carefully examined, will materially contribute to a clear understanding of what is to be said. A few explanations may be necessary, and hence are here given.

The large square, marked by heavy black lines, indicates the base of the edifice, which covers about thirteen acres of ground, equal to about four ordinary blocks of our city, including their streets. The darkened triangular mass represents the body of the pyramid, showing the slopes of the sides as they rise to a point at the summit. The lines on the outside mark the original size, as covered with polished casing-stones, all of which have been quarried off by the Moslems, to build and ornament the mosques and houses of Cairo, or to be burnt for lime. About thirty feet of the original edifice has also disappeared from the top, leaving perhaps twenty-four feet square of level space, from which the strongest man cannot throw a stone, or shoot an arrow, far enough to fall clear of the base. Even with so much of the summit gone, it is still more than double the height of the highest steeple or tower in Philadelphia, and higher than the highest known steeple or tower in the world.

The elevation shows the pyramid cut in half, from north to south, in order to give a view of the interior. As here seen, the spectator is looking from east to west. There are no known openings but those which appear in these open and unshaded spaces. The dark square toward the top (U) indicates an imaginary room which is believed to exist, but not yet discovered.

The only entrance into the edifice, as left by the builders, is that low and narrow square tube, which begins high up on the north side, and runs obliquely down to an unfinished room in the solid rock, about one hundred feet below the levelled surface on which the pyramid stands. The size of this entrance passage is not quite four feet high, and a little over three feet five inches wide. A man needs to stoop considerably to pass through it, and to take heed to his steps on account of the steep incline, originally finished as smooth as a slate, from top to bottom.

The first upward passage is directly over the entrance-tube, and is of the same general size and character. It follows the same direction from north to south, and conducts to a high, long and beautifully finished opening, whose floor-line is continuous with the passage of ascent to it. This is the Grand Gallery, twenty-eight feet high, each of whose sides is built of seven courses of overlapping stones. It is covered by thirty-six large stones stretching across the top. It is a little over eighteen hundred and eighty-two inches long, and suddenly terminates against an end wall, which leans inward. The further opening is low and small again, leading into a sort of narrow anteroom, in which a double and heavy granite block hangs from grooves in the side walls.

Then follows another low entrance leading into what is called the King's Chamber, the highest and largest known room in the edifice. In this chamber stands the only article of furniture in the pyramid, the celebrated granite Coffer. Above this room are shown what are called the chambers of construction, indicating how the builders arranged to keep the weight of the superincumbent mass from crushing in the ceiling of the King's Chamber, which ceiling consists of nine powerful blocks of granite, stretching from one side to the other. The dark or crossed shadings about this chamber indicate the stones to be granite, all the rest of the building not so marked is of light limestone. This room is an oblong square, four hundred and twelve inches long, two hundred and six broad and two hundred and thirty high. It is ventilated by two tubes, running from it to the outer surface.

Directly under the Grand Gallery, and running in the same direction from north to south, is a horizontal passage, which starts on a level with the entrance into the Grand Gallery, and leads to what is called the Queen's Chamber. The floor of this room, if floor it may be called, measures two hundred and five by two hundred and twenty-six inches, and stands on the twenty-fifth course of masonry, as the King's Chamber stands on the fiftieth course. It has a pointed arch ceiling. Though excellently finished, this room has neither ornament nor furniture. There is a line marked evenly around its sides at the height of the passage of entrance, and a remarkable niche in its east wall, the top of which is twenty-five inches across and twenty-five inches south from the vertical centre of the wall into which it is cut. This room also has two tubes leading from it, only recently discovered, which the builders left concealed by a thin scale over each. They are cut regularly, and approach inward through the walls to within one inch of the inner surface, which was left as though no such openings existed back of it. Whether these tubes extend to the outer surface has not been ascertained.

Nearly three feet from the beginning of the Grand Gallery, on the west side, is a torn and ragged opening, in which is the gaping mouth of a strange well, running irregularly and somewhat tortuously down through the masonry and original rock, till it strikes the main entrance a short way above the subterranean chamber. Nearly half the way down it expands into a rough grotto or wide bulge in the opening, making a large irregular subterranean bowl.

Below the entrance passage, and a little to the west of it, the dark and rugged opening shown represents the hole made by one of the Mohammedan caliphs, about A.D. 825, who thus cut into the pyramid in search of treasures, not knowing that there was an open passage not far above.

The small black squares represented at the corners of the base indicate the peculiar sockets, cut eight inches into the living rock, into which the foundation corner-stones were set. These are characteristics of the Great Pyramid, in which it differs from all others, and are of special value, in the present ruinous condition

of the edifice, in ascertaining the exact original
corners and the precise lengths of the sides.

The encompassing circle, drawn to the radius
of the pyramid's height, indicates the mathematical idea to which the whole building is
constructed; the length of the four sides of
the square base being the same as the circumference described by a sphere, of which the
vertical height is the radius. It shows the
edifice in that remarkable feature, to wit, a
practical *squaring of the circle.*

The smaller pyramids below represent the
next in size and age to the Great Pyramid.
They are introduced for no other purpose than
to show the difference of interior between them
and it; on which difference an argument is
founded to prove them mere ignorant imitations
of the Great Pyramid, and not at all to be
classed with it in intellectuality and design.

The hieroglyphics are reproductions of the
cartouches of the two kings, Shufu and Nem-
Shufu, who occupied the throne at the time the
Great Pyramid was built. They were discovered by Colonel Howard Vyse, in 1837,
roughly painted on the undressed sides of the
stones in the upper chambers of construction,
which were never opened until he forced a
way up to them.

THE HISTORY.

There is no known time within our historic periods when this pyram'd was not famous. Herodotus, the so-called Father of History, as early as 445 B.C., made a personal examination of it, and devoted some most interesting paragraphs to it. It was then already considered very ancient. Traditional accounts of its erection he gathered through an interpreter from an Egyptian priest, and these he has recorded with much particularity. His own appreciation of the structure, and of the causeway over which the materials were conveyed, was that of wonder and admiration.*

Homer does not seem to make any allusion to it, perhaps for the reason that it had no connection with mythology, or with any of his heroes.

Eratosthenes (236 B.C.), Diodorus Siculus (60 B.C.), and Strabo and Pliny (about the beginning of our era), all wrote of it. The latter, in referring to the Pyramids, also says, " The authors who have written upon them are Herodotus, Euhemerus, Durius Samius, Aristagoras, Dionysius, Artemedorus, Alex-

---

* See Rawlinson's Herodotus, Book II, chap. 124, vol. 2, pp. 169-176.

ander, Polyhistor, Butorides, Autisthenes, Demetrius, Demoteles, and Apion."*

But though the Great Pyramid has been standing in its place for 4000 years, it is only within a very recent period that there has been any rational appreciation of it. For 3000 years of its existence, up to the time of the mediæval Caliph Al Mamoun, no mortal man, perhaps, ever penetrated into its upper passages and main openings. Certainly, for many centuries before him, it was completely closed up, no entrance to it being known any more to any human being.

This son of Haroun Al Raschid of the "Arabian Nights," flattered and almost worshipped as a god, was so wrought upon by the romancers and fabulists of his court that he was led to believe the Great Pyramid crowded full of precious treasures. All the dazzling riches, jewels, medicines, charms, and sciences of Sheddad Ben Ad, the Mussulman's great antediluvian king of the earth, were made to glitter before the avaricious fancy of Al Mamoun. He therefore set his hosts at work to quarry out an opening into the wonderful treasure-house, full of astonishing riches in-

---

* Nat. Hist., tom. 36, sec. 16.

deed, but not of the sort of which he was dreaming.

With the crude instruments and poor knowl-edge which his hordes possessed, it proved no easy task to cut through that grand masonry. Again and again the thing was pronounced impossible. But Mohammedan fanaticism and tyranny proved equal to the undertaking; not, however, without straining everything to the very utmost, and Al Mamoun's own power to the point of revolution. The excavation was driven in full one hundred feet, with every-thing solid up to that point. Having expended all this labor to no effect, all further effort was about to be abandoned, when a singular, per-haps providential, occurrence served to reani-mate exertion. The sound of a falling stone in some open space not far beyond them was heard, which incited them to dig and bore on, till presently they broke through into the reg-ular passage-way. They struck this tube just where the first ascending passage forks off from the descending one. The stone which had fallen was one which hung in the top of the entrance passage, quite concealing the fact of another and upward way. But the newly uncovered passage they found stopped by a heavy stone portcullis, fitted into it from above as tight as a cork in the mouth of a bottle. It was impossible to remove it. It remains there still. Al Mamoun caused his men to dig and blast around it. But even beyond the portcullis, the whole passage was filled up with great stones from top to bottom. Removing one, the next slid down in its place; and so another and another, each of which was removed, till at length the entire upward avenue was freed from obstructions. Up went the bearded crew, shouting the name of Allah, in full confidence that the promised treasures were now within their grasp. "Up," as Prof. Smyth describes it, " up no less than one hundred and ten feet of the steep incline, crouched hands and knees and chin together, through a passage of royally polished lime-stone, but only forty-seven inches high and forty-one broad, they had painfully to crawl, with their torches burning low." Thence they emerged into the Grand Gallery, long and tall, seven times as high as the passage through which they came, empty, however, and darker than night. Still the way was narrow and steep, only six feet wide at any point, and contracted to three at the floor, though too high for the power of their smoky lights to illuminate. Up and up the smooth and long ascending floor-line the marauders pushed

their slippery and doubtful way, till near the
end of the Grand Gallery. Then they clam-
bered over a three-foot step; then bowed their
heads beneath a low doorway, bounded on all
sides with awful blocks of frowning red granite; and then leaped without further hin-
drance into the Grand Chamber, the first to
enter since the Great Pyramid was built.*

---

* It is barely possible that there was once a forced entrance
into the upper parts of the Great Pyramid, long before the
Mohammedan times. At the beginning of the Grand Gallery
there is a missing ramp-stone, which once covered the mouth
of the well. This ramp-stone seems to have been forced out
from below upwards, as a fragment of it is still seen adhering
to the next stone, held by the firm cement of the joint. Hence
it is surmised that some fanatics of the dynasties of Ethiopic
intruders, or the Persian conquerors after them, forcibly entered in search of treasures by means of the well, and then
closed up the entrance again to conceal what they had done.
This is thought the more probable, as the other pyramids,
which were used as royal tombs, seem to have been entered and
rifled at some remote period of the past. But when we consider
some of the high prophetic meanings connected with the
Grand Gallery, and of that well out of which it takes its beginning, we would rather infer that the builders themselves broke
out that ramp-stone, or sealed on that fragment in a way indicative of violent bursting out from below, as part of the great
intention and teaching of the mighty fabric. This is the more
probable, (1) because no part of that missing ramp-stone has
ever been found; (2) because of the extraordinary difficulty of
breaking away such a stone from within the well; and (3)
the difficulty of, and absence of motive for, a removal of the
stone if broken in by the supposed marauders. Hence we
conclude that the situation was intentionally so left by the

A noble chamber did these maddened Moslems also find it, clean and garnished, every surface of polished red granite, and everything indicative of master builders. But the coveted gold and treasures were not there. Nothing was there but black and solemn emptiness. There stood a solitary stone chest, indeed, fashioned out of a single block, polished within and without, and sonorous as a bell, but open, lidless, and empty as the space around it. The caliph was astounded. His quarriers muttered their anathemas over their deception into such enormous, unrequited, and fruitless labors. Nor could Al Mamoun quiet the outbreaking indignation toward him and his courtiers, except by one of those saintly frauds in which Mohammedanism is so facile. He commanded the discontents to go dig at a spot which he indicated, where they soon came upon a sum of gold, exactly equal to the wages claimed for their work, which gold he had himself secretly deposited at the place. When it was found, he could not repress his astonishment that those mighty kings before the flood were so full of inspiration as to be able to count so

builders themselves, and that no one after them had entered the upper parts of the Great Pyramid prior to Al Mamoun's hordes.

truly what it would cost in Arab labor to break open their pyramid!

But the great mysterious structure was now open. Henceforward any one with interest and courage enough to attempt it might enter, examine, study, and find out what he could.

For centuries the Arabians went in and out betimes, when able to overcome their superstitious fears. Some of their marvellous tales of small miracles and vulgar wonders have been put on record. But apart from the mere fact of the forcible entrance by Al Mamoun, it is agreed that scarcely a shred of their testimony is at all credible.*

---

* The principal Arab writers who give accounts of the Pyramids are Abou Ma Sher (died 272 of the Hegira), Ebn Khordadbeh (died about 300 of same era), Abou Rihan Mohammed (about 430), Masoudi (died 345), Abou Abdullah Mohammed (died 454), Abd Alatif (born 557), Shehab Eddin Ahmed (died about 745), Ebn Abd Al Hokm Makizi (died about 845), Soyuti (died 911), etc. The dates given are those of the Hegira, to which add 622 to give the year of our era.

The worth of what these men have recorded, may be learned from the following testimonies :

" The authority of Arab writers is not always to be relied on."—SIR GARDINER WILKINSON, *Murray's Handbook*, 1867, p. 168.

" The only fact which seems to be established by the Eastern authors to whom we have now referred (the Arabians), is the opening of the Great Pyramid by Al Mamoun ; and even of that, no distinct or rational account exists."—COL. HOWARD VYSE.

Prof. John Greaves (1637) quotes from some of these writers,

We must therefore depend on the explorations and accounts of the more observant, appreciative, and philosophic European mind for
our knowledge of the Great Pyramid.   In some
instances, however, the case is not much im-
proved.   Sir John Mandeville, perhaps the
greatest English traveller of the middle ages,
who spent thirty-three years in wanderings
through the East, visited Egypt and the Pyramids about A.D. 1350, and has left us a theory
concerning them, but confesses that he was
afraid to enter them, because they were re-
puted to be full of serpents !*

The earliest writer of modern times from
whom we have any scientific data with regard
to the Great Pyramid is Mr. John Greaves,
Savilian Professor of Astronomy in the Uni-

---

and adds, " Thus far the Arabians, which traditions of theirs
are little better than a romance "

Professor Smyth, after trying and testing the whole body of
accounts, says, " We find ourselves standing again just where
Prof. Greaves stood in 1637, obliged to reject every rag of testimony from the followers of the false prophet."—*Antiquity of
Intellectual Man*," p. 277.

* Other European authors who have given accounts of the
Pyramids are Cyriacus, A.D. 1440; Breydenbach, 1486;
Bellonius, 1553; Johannes Helfricus, 1565; Lawrence Alder-
sey, 1586; Jeane Palerma, 1581; Prosper Alpinus, 1591;
Baumgarten, 1594; Sandys, 1610; Pietro Della Vale, 1616;
De Villamont, 1618; Rabbi Benjamin, 1633; most of whom
themselves visited the Pyramids.

versity of Oxford. At his own private expense
he left London in the spring of 1637 for the
special purpose of thoroughly exploring these
ancient edifices, and in 1646 published his
Pyramidographia, giving the results of his
laborious observations and measurements,
which are of particular worth in obtaining an
accurate knowledge of this subject. But he
was soon followed by other explorers, French,
English, Dutch, Germans, and Italians.*

Special additions were made to the stock of
Pyramid information by Nathaniel Davison,
British Consul at Algiers (1763), who resided
three years in Egypt, frequently visited the
Great Pyramid, discovered the first of those
chambers of construction above the so-called
King's Chamber, drew a profile of the original
casing-stones, and made the first diagram of
the supposed appearance of this pillar when it
stood complete.†

---

* Among these may be mentioned De Monconys (1647),
Thevenot (1655), Melton (1661), Vausleb (1664), Kircher
(1666), Lebrun (1674), Maillet (1692–1708), De Careri (1693),
Lucas (1699), Veryard (1701), Quatremere (1701), Egmont
(1709), Perizonius (1711), Pere Sicard (1715), Shaw (1721),
Norden (1737), Pococke (1743), Dr. Perry (1743), Four-
mount (1755), Niebuhr (1761).

† The results of Davison's labors are contained in the
Memoirs of Rev. Robert Walpole, and are alluded to at some
length in vol. 19 of the *Quarterly Review.* Other writers on the

When Napoleon was engaged with his military operations in Egypt (1799), the French *savants* who accompanied his expedition also did important service in furnishing a knowledge of the Great Pyramid. They surveyed the ground. They determined the value of the location in trigonometrical relations. They found two of the " encastrements," or incisions in the rock, meant to serve as sockets for the original corner-stones of the foundation. Their observations and mostly very accurate measurements, with cuts, engravings, and descriptions of the Great Pyramid, were subsequently published, in large and elegant form.*

Very splendid contributions to our knowledge of the subject were made by Colonel (afterwards General) Howard Vyse in his three large royal octavo volumes, containing the results of seven months' labor, with a hundred or more assistants, in exploring and measuring the

---

subject after him, were Bruce (1768), L'Abbe De Binos (1777), Savary (1777), Volney (1783), Browne (1792–98), Devon (1799).

* See Colonel Coutelle's remarks (1801), and particularly M. Jomard's descriptions (1801).

Other writers are Hamilton (1801), Dr. Whitman (1801), Dr. Wilson (1805), M Caviglia (1817), M. Belzoni (1817), Signore Athanasi (1817), Dr. Richardson (1817), Mr. Webster (1827), Wilkinson (1831), Mr. St. John (1832), Captain Scott and Mr. Agnew (1837).

Pyramids, in 1837. It is he especially who, at the expense of a large fortune, laid the foundations for some of the most brilliant and important developments to be found in all the scientific world of our century. He reopened the ragged hole driven into the stupendous edifice by the semi-savages of Al Mamoun, and made some others himself, part of which were equally fruitless. He uncovered again the two indented sockets of the north base corners. He discovered and reopened the remarkable ventilating tubes of the King's Chamber. He cut a way through the masonry above that chamber, and found four other openings besides the one discovered by Davison. He found in those recesses various quarry-marks in red paint, proving that writing was known and practiced in the fourth Egyptian dynasty. Among these marks were the *cartouches* of the co-sovereign brothers who reigned at the time the Great Pyramid was built. He also found some of the original casing-stones still fast in their places, as well as portions of a splendid pavement which once surrounded the edifice. In addition to these new discoveries he fully confirmed what had been ascertained before, and served to bring this marvellous structure within the sphere of modern scientific investi-

gation. Through him, Sir John Herschel es-
poused the belief that the Great Pyramid
possesses a truly astronomical character, and
that its narrow tubic entrance pointed to some
polar star, from which the date of the building is determinable. At Vyse's instance this
astronomer made the calculation, and found
the pointing to indicate the same period of
time which, on other and independent data,
had been concluded as the period of the Great
Pyramid's building. And thus was laid the
basis from which a new theory of this marvellous pillar has sprung.

The Modern Scientific Theory.

Taking what had thus been produced with
regard to the Great Pyramid, John Taylor
(one of the firm of Taylor & Hessey, publishers
of the *London Magazine*, and subsequently
of the firm of Taylor & Wallace, publishers
to the University of London), undertook to
wrestle with the questions: *Why was this
pyramid built? And who built it?* Canvass-
ing the whole problem in the light of history,
religion, and science, he came to some very
surprising conclusions, involving an altogether
new departure in Pyramid investigations, and
enunciating a number of facts with regard to

the mathematical features of the Great Pyramid, which once were ridiculed, but are now generally admitted as demonstrably true. In 1859 he published a small volume, in which he proposed " to recover a lost leaf in the world's history," and gave his processes and the results. Without having seen the Great Pyramid, but on the basis of the facts recorded by others, he gave it as his theory and conviction that the real architects of this edifice were not Egyptians, but men of quite another faith and branch of the human family, who, by an impulse and commission from heaven, and by the special aid of the Most High, induced and superintended the erection of that mighty structure, as a memorial for long after times, to serve as a witness of inspiration, and of the truth and purposes of God, over against the falsities and corruptions of a degenerate and ever degenerating world. In other words, he claimed to find, in the shape, arrangements, measures, and various indications of the Great Pyramid, an intellectuality and numerical knowledge of grand cosmical phenomena of earth and heavens, which neither Egypt nor any of the nations possessed, or could even understand, from a thousand years ago, back to the origin of nations.

This was a bold, striking, and far-reaching presentation, and one well worthy of the attention of the thinkers of our age, both religious and philosophical. Very few, however, paid much attention to his vigorous little book. Yet the grounds on which he proceeded and the processes employed, were so purely within the domain of science, and hence so easy of decisive refutation if not true, that scientists could hardly be fair to their profession without some investigation of the matter. Sir John Herschel was certainly much impressed with some of the results and conclusions brought out by Mr. Taylor, and also very powerfully used them in his papers on the standard of British measures, over against the falsely founded system of metres, originated by the French infidels and communists.

A few years after the appearance of Mr. Taylor's book, it arrested the attention and enlisted the interest of Prof. C. Piazzi Smyth, of Edinburgh, Astronomer Royal for Scotland. Having investigated the subject to some extent, he presented a paper to the Royal Society of Edinburgh, in 1864, giving the results of his researches and calculations to test the truth of some of Mr. Taylor's startling presentations, and setting forth his acquiescence in many of the details, though on somewhat different grounds. These investigations and conclusions of Prof. Smyth were published the same year, in his book, *Our Inheritance in the Great Pyramid*, a new, revised, and enlarged edition of which was published in 1874. This book, in its revised form, is perhaps the best from which to get a full impression, within a limited space, of the nature and grounds of the modern scientific theory on the subject.

The better to satisfy himself, and in order to clear up some matters of uncertainty in the case, Prof. Smyth, at his own expense, went to Egypt, and spent the winter and spring of 1865, devoting the time to the work of testing, by the best modern scientific appliances, what others had recorded concerning this pyramid. To facilitate his operations, he and his brave wife took up their abode in some of the tombs in the vicinity, where they lived and worked from the first of January to the end of April. The results of these self-denying labors were given to the public in three brilliant volumes, in 1867, entitled, *Life and Work at the Great Pyramid*, with a sequel in the year following, *On the Antiquity of Intellectual Man*.

From the publication of these very valuable books, various discussions in learned societies and the public prints followed; new investigators entered upon the subject; and many converts to the new theory were made. A number of able papers appeared, confirming and enlarging what had previously been deduced, and fully supporting the scientifically grounded and growing belief that this venerable pillar has about it something more than a mere tomb for some rich and ambitious old Pharaoh, and something infinitely more than was ever in the power of the Egyptians to originate, or even to understand. In other words, that it was designed and erected under the special guidance and direction of God, and bears a somewhat similar relation to the physical universe which the Bible bears to the spiritual.

Upon first blush such a theory would seem to be the very height of fanaticism and nonsense. And so a few, in their offended conceit and prejudice, rather than from any solid scientific reasons, have regarded it. As commonly, in all such cases, the power of coarse ridicule has been brought to bear against it; but thus far no candid and thorough attempt has been made to overcome the many solid and outstanding evidences on which it rests. Goodsir, in his volume on *Ethnic Inspiration*, has

justly said, "The scientific symbolism of that
world's wonder now stands nearly disclosed
to view, resting on its own independent basis
of proof, which is not only vouched for, but
defended by advocates undeniably competent
to their work, and as yet occupying inexpugn-
ably their ground." Every attack upon it
thus far has resulted in such signal failure as
the more to confirm it.

It is of course impossible here to go into all
the particulars, processes, and scientific induc-
tions on which this theory rests. These are
given, in all their surprising force, in the able
original works to which I have referred, and
to which I direct all who wish to sift the matter
thoroughly or inform themselves fully. Mathematicians and scientists will find enough there
to call all their knowledge into play, and to
occupy their inquiries and skill for as much
time as they may have to give. My office is
of a much simpler and easier sort. A brief
résumé of the principal facts, to enable those
who hear me to form some fair opinion of the
matter, is all that I propose, feeling that if I
can succeed in this, I shall have done something of worth in making known the wonders
of wisdom so long ago treasured up in the
Great Pyramid of Gizeh.

THE VARIOUS PYRAMIDS.

There are numerous pyramids in Egypt. Including all sizes and forms, perhaps three dozen may still be found. They belong to different ages, from B.C. 2170 down to B.C. 1800. Externally, they all are more or less of the same general form. A few are not much inferior in dimensions, materials, and outward finish to the Great Pyramid itself. But there is one, the northernmost of the line, which has ever held the pre-eminence, and which has always been regarded with the greatest interest. The sacred books of the Hindoos speak of three pyramids in Egypt, and they describe this as " the golden mountain," and the other two as mountains of silver and less valuable material. By a sort of intuition, all nations and tongues unite in recognizing this one as *The Great Pyramid*. It covers the most space. It occupies the most commanding position. It is built with most skill and perfection of workmanship. And its summit rises higher heavenward than that of any other.

This greatest of the pyramids is also the oldest of them. Lepsius says, " The builders of the Great Pyramid seem to assert their right to form the commencement of monumental history." "To the Pyramid of Cheops the first link of our whole monumental history is fastened immovably, not for Egyptian, but for universal history." Prof. Smyth holds that "the world has no material and contemporary record of intellectual man earlier than the Great Pyramid." Beckett Denison agrees that this is "the earliest and largest of all the pyramids." Hales in his *Analysis*, Sharpe in his *History of Egypt*, Bunsen in his *Egypt's Place in History*, and the best authors in general, make the same representations. There is no evidence on earth, known to man, that ever a true pyramid was built before the erection of the Great Pyramid of Gizeh.

Here, then, is a fact to start with which utterly confounds the ordinary laws in human affairs. The arts of man left to himself, never attain perfection at once. At all times and in all countries, there is invariably a series of crude attempts and imperfect beginnings first, and thence a gradual advance from a less perfect to a more complete. Styles of architecture do not spring into existence like Minerva from the brain of Jupiter, fullgrown and perfect from the start. But here all ordinary laws are reversed, and the classic dream finds reality. As with the beginning of our race,

so with the pyramids, the most perfect is first
and what comes after is deteriorate. The
Great Pyramid comes upon the scene and
maintains its grand superiority forever, without any preceding type of its class whence
the idea was evolved. Renan says, "It has no
archaic epoch." Osburn says, "It bursts upon
us at once in the flower of its highest perfection." It suddenly takes its place in the world
in all its matchless magnificence, "without
father, without mother," and as clean apart
from all evolution as if it had dropped down
from the unknown heavens. We can no more
account for its appearance in this fashion on
ordinary principles than we can account for
the being of Adam without a special Divine
intervention.

This pyramid once in existence, it is not
difficult to account for all the rest. Having
been taught how to build it, and with the grand
model ever before them, men could easily build
more. But how to get the original with its
transcendent superiority to all others is the
trouble. The theory of Mr. Taylor and Prof.
Smyth would admirably solve the riddle; but
apart from that, there is no knowledge of man
by which it can be solved. People may guess
and suppose; but they can tell us nothing.

The evidences also are, that the whole family of Egyptian pyramids, and there are no others, is made up of mere blind and bungling imitations of the Great Pyramid. They take its general form, but they every one miss its intellectuality and take on none of their own. None of them has any upper openings or chambers; and the reason is furnished in what Al Mamoun on making his forced entrance found in the Great Pyramid, to wit, the fact that its upward passage-way was stopped by its builders, filled up, hidden, and then for the first time discovered. These upper openings, though the main features of the Great Pyramid's interior, were wholly unknown to the copyists, and hence were not copied. The downward passage and the subterranean chamber were known, and could be inspected; hence these features appear in all the pyramids. It would be difficult to conceive more conclusive internal evidences of mere imitation, or of the certainty that the Great Pyramid is the real original of all pyramids. All the rest are but vulgar and unmeaning piles of stones in comparison with it.

FORM AND PROPORTIONS.

A building having a square base and its four

sides equally sloped inwards to a single point at the top is a pyramid. There may be other and various pyramidal forms, but they are not true pyramids. In stone architecture such a figure requires the edifice to be solid, or mainly so, and can furnish very little internal space for any practical use. It is therefore a style of building which is itself something peculiar and quite unfitted to any of the ordinary purposes for which man erects edifices.

But not all pyramids have the same relative proportions or degree of slope in their sides. In this respect the Great Pyramid stands alone among all other pyramids or buildings on earth. Plato says, that "God perpetually geometrizes," and this pyramid presents a clear and solid geometric figure with all its proportions conformed to each other.

Science has frequently alluded to a certain triplicity or triunity of nature, assuming something of the character of a law of creation, and traceable as a sort of pervading analogy of Providence. Poets, those close observers and portrayers of nature, have likewise referred to it. The crust of the earth is composed of a grand triplicity of primary, secondary, and tertiary stratifications. Compte beheld the laws of mind as made up of supernatural, metaphysical, and positive stages in mental evolution. Burke thought he saw a parallel between mythology and geology, and classified the former according to the three stages of the earth's formation. A modern chemist reduces all the properties of matter to attraction, repulsion, and vitality. And a late attempt to give "a basic outline of universology," comprises all things in unism, duism, and trinism. Without accepting these things as settled truths, they yet serve to show a primary something, which, to the most observant minds, bespeaks an original triplicity, putting itself forth as a rudimental law. And if the Great Pyramid was really intended to symbolize the universe, we would also expect to find in it some recognition of this triplicity or triunity. Accordingly we do find this to be the fundamental figure of the Great Pyramid, which is at the same time the geometrical skeleton of the earth, if not also of the whole physical and spiritual universe.

It was a great achievement of our science to ascertain that the earth is a revolving globe. But this spherity is the mere clothing of a mathematical figure to which it is formed. As a revolving body, the earth has an *axis of rotation*, that is, it makes all its revolutions in one and the same unvarying direction, indicating a primary straight line through its centre to its poles. Using this as a base line, which it is in fact, and drawing two equal lines from the surface at the poles to the highest point of surface at the equator, the result is one of the simplest compound figures in geometry—*a triangle*—just what we have in the outline figure of the Great Pyramid, and in each of its four faces.

Examining this figure more closely, still other remarkable properties appear. Viewed as a triangle, if we square its base line, as squared in fact in the Great Pyramid, and add together the lengths of the four sides, we have the exact equal of a circle drawn with the vertical height for a radius. In other words, we have here a figure of the framework of the earth, and that figure possessed of the proportion which is known to mathematicians as the π proportion,—thus presenting a practical solution of that puzzling problem which has cracked so many mediæval and modern brains, to wit, the quadrature of the circle. Hence John Taylor says of the builders of the Great Pyramid, that "they imagined the earth to be a sphere, and as they knew that the radius of a circle must bear a certain proportion to its circumference, they built a four-sided pyramid of such a height in proportion to its base, that its perpendicular would be the radius of a sphere equal to the perimeter of the base."

The other pyramids have the same general form copied after this, but these mathematical proportions and signs of high intellectuality appear nowhere but in the Great Pyramid. And when Jomard says, " The pyramids have preserved to us the certain type of the size of the terrestrial globe," he utters a great truth, but what is not true in any definite measure save of the Great Pyramid.

PYRAMID NUMBERS.

The peculiar figure and shape of the Great Pyramid fixes a certain system of numbers. It has five corners : four equal corners at the base and one unique corner at the summit. Hence it has five sides ; four equal triangular sides and the square under-side on which it stands. Here is an emphatic count of *fives* doubled into the convenient decimal. This count is so inherent and marked as to be a strong characteristic, calling for the number *five*, and multiples, powers and geometrical proportions of it, as loudly as stones can be made to speak.

From this also it would seem to have its name. Though different authors have sought to derive this word from the Greek, Arabic, and other sources, the evidence is rather that it came direct from the builders of the edifice, and was meant to describe it in the common language then used in the country. The nearest to that language is the Coptic. And in the ancient Coptic, *pyr* means *division*, the same as *peres* in Daniel's interpretation of the handwriting on the wall ; and *met* means *ten*. Chevalier Bunsen, without thought of combining them for the derivation of the word *pyramid*, gives these words separately and affixes to them these significations.* And putting them together—*pyr-met*—we have the name given to this structure. And that name, in the language of the ancient Egyptians, means *the division of ten.*

Accordingly a system of *fiveness* runs through the Great Pyramid and its measure references. Counting five times five courses of the masonry from the base upwards we are brought to the floor of the so-called Queen's Chamber. The measures of that chamber all answer to a standard of five times five inches.

---

* See Egypt's Place in History, vol. i, p. 477, and vol. iv, p. 107.

It is characterized by a deep sunken niche in one of its walls, which niche is three times five feet high, consisting of five strongly marked stories, the topmost five times five inches across, and its inner edge just five times five inches from the perpendicular centre of the wall into which it is cut. So if we count five times five courses higher, or ten times five from the base, the last brings us on the floor of the King's Chamber. That chamber contains just ten fives of cubic space and is just ten five times the size of the mysterious granite Coffer which stands in it. Each of its walls is finished with five horizontal courses of polished granite stones. The number of these stones in all is four fives multiplied by five. Above it are five chambers of construction; and the Coffer itself has five solid external sides.

This intense *fiveness* could not have been accidental, and likewise corresponds with the arrangements of God, both in nature and revelation. Note the fiveness of termination to each limb of the human body, the five senses, the five books of Moses, the twice five precepts of the Decalogue. But this is not all. Science now tells us that the diameter of the earth at the poles is five hundred millions of units, about the length of our inches. Five times

five of these units or inches is the twice ten
millionth part of the earth's axis of rotation.
Ten times ten of these units or inches counted
for a day, when divided into the united lengths
of the Great Pyramid's four sides, give the
exact number of days in the true year. As
near as science has been able to determine the
mean density of the earth (5.70), five cubic
inches of it weighs just the fifty times fiftieth
part of the Coffer's contents of water at a temperature of one-fifth of the distance which the
mercury rises from the freezing to the boiling-
point.

Nine is another number very specially marked
in the Great Pyramid, particularly in its sun-
ward portions and tendencies. Its practical
shaping is nine to ten. For every ten feet that
its corners retreat diagonally inwards in the
process of building they rise upward or sun-
ward nine feet.* At high noon the sun shines

---

* From this 10,9 shape of the Great Pyramid there results
also important confirmation of the measurements of the base
side and height. "The side angle computed from it amounts to
51° 50′ 39.1″; the π angle being 51° 51′ 14.3″; and the angle
from Mr. Taylor's interpretation of Herodotus, or to the effect
of the Great Pyramid having been built to represent an area on
the side equal to the height squared 51° 49′ 25″. The vertical
heights in pyramid (earth-commensurated) inches are at the
same time, using the same base side length for them all by the
10,9 hypothesis, 5811; by the π hypothesis 5813; and by the

on all five of its corners and four of its sides,
counting nine of its most characteristic parts.
The Grand Gallery is roofed with four times
nine stones, and the main chamber with
exactly nine. And here again we have a
nature reference which nations have expended
millions to ascertain. The vertical height of
the Great Pyramid multiplied by 10 to the 9th
power (10^9) tells the mean distance of the sun
from the earth, that is one thousand million
times the pyramid's height, or 91,840,000
miles.

The sun-distance used to be put down by
astronomy at nearly 96,000,000 miles. Later
computations, at the opposition of Mars in
1862, reduced this estimate to between ninety-
one and ninety-three millions. The results of

Herodotus-Taylor hypothesis 5807." The nearness to identity
of the results of such diverse methods amply proves that the
assumed measure of each base side, by taking the mean of all
the practical measurements between the sockets, cannot be far
from the true measure laid out by the architects, and hence a
just foundation on which to proceed in any calculations or conclusions that may result. Those who are disposed to rid themselves of such conclusions on the ground that we do not know
with sufficient accuracy what is the length of the pyramid's base
sides, ought to consider these remarkable facts, and meet them
in a fair and scientific way, or else admit that there is no such
vitiating uncertainty as they too fondly assume without being
able practically or by any process to prove that our figures are
false.

the observations of the transit of Venus in
1874 have confirmed these lower figures,
making the limit of uncertainty to lie between
ninety-one and ninety-two and a half millions.
Taking the mean of the estimates as the best
that modern science has been able to present,
we have a very close agreement with the Great
Pyramid's symbolizations. And when science
has once definitely settled the point, there is
now every indication that the figures will agree
precisely with what was not only known to
the architects of this pyramid, but was by
them imperishably memorialized in stone more
than 4000 years ago!

All this proves not only intelligent design
on the part of these builders, but an acquaintance with nature, and a genius for the expression of nature's truths in the forms and
measures of a plain, simple, and enduring
structure, which any less attainment than that
of our greatest living astronomers and *savants*
could not so much as understand.

SIZE OF THE GREAT PYRAMID.

The opinion was given by Lepsius, and from
him has been largely accepted as a law in
Egyptian pyramid building, that each king,
when he came to the throne, began to excavate

a subterranean chamber with an inclined passage, which chamber was meant for his tomb;
the first year he covered it with a few squared
blocks of stone, the next added more, and so
continued till he died, leaving it to his successor to finish and close the edifice. Hence
the size of each pyramid would depend upon
the accident of the duration of the king's life.
Perhaps it was so after pyramids came to be
a fashion, though some long-lived kings have
only small pyramids. But it is very certain
that the Great Pyramid did not *grow* in this
way. Its whole character was calculated and
determined beforehand. The drafts of its
architects still exist, graven in the rocks, as
Job wished that his words might be in order
to last forever. There they are in the immediate vicinity of the great building, the pro-
jection of whose shape and features, without
and within, they still show to every one who
wishes to examine them. By them it is proven
that the whole structure in its angles and mathematical proportions was contemplated and
designed from the start.* Besides, the subter-

---

* "These azimuth trenches are a sort of large open ditches
spread about here and there on the surface of the hill, before
the eastern face of the Great Pyramid, and not very noticeable
except for their relative angles in a horizontal plane; for these
gave me the idea at first sight of being strangely similar to the

ranean chamber of the Great Pyramid which
this "law" would require to be finished first

---

dominant angles of the exterior of the Great Pyramid.   To
determine whether this idea was true or not, I determined to
measure all the angles rather carefully."   " Most happily, toc,
every part of them which has to enter into the measurement,
still exist visibly and tangibly; so that good painstaking
modern observation is perfectly able of itself, either to prove
or disprove what has just been advanced," *i.e.*, their correspondence to the angle of the foot of the Great Pyramid.—" Life
and Work at Great Pyramid," vol. ii, p. 125, vol. iii, p. 28.

" For several reasons I consider these trenches have been originally incised for instructing the masons in the exact angular
character of the very mathematically formed building they were
engaged on, and while the work was in progress."—" Antiquity
of Intellectual Man," p. 192.

" If you take the Great Pyramid as it was when in masonry
progress or without its final casing film, and if from the centre
of the then base you draw its proportion π circle, the conjoined
axes of north and south azimuth trenches will form a tangent
to that circle at its most protuberant point in front of the
middle east side.   And further, if from the points toward the
north and south extremities of the east side of base where the
π circle cuts into the area of the base you draw rectangular
offsets from that side eastward, these offsets will be found to
define the places of the admirably square cut outer ends of
both north and south azimuth trenches with as much accuracy
as the present standing and broken sides of the pyramid admit
of in their measurement."—MR. W. PETRIE, quoted by PROF.
SMYTH.

Besides these trenches there is also a system of inclined tun-
nels cut into the rock of the hill, which some have taken to be
the remains or the commencement of another pyramid of small
size.   But Prof. Smyth found them arranged on the same
principles contained in the Great Pyramid, and only in it.
He says of them: "There is a long descending entrance passage, an upward and opposite rising passage from the middle of
that like the Great Pyramid's first ascending passage; then the

is just that part which never was finished at
all. It is only half cut out,—a mere pit without a bottom. Herodotus also gathered from
the Egyptians themselves that ten years were
spent in building preparatory works, which are
hardly less remarkable and elaborate than the
pyramid itself, and that everything was organized on an immense scale, keeping 100,000
men continually at work, relaying them every
three months. Furthermore, all the search-
ings into this pyramid have failed to reveal
any signs of the patching of one year's work
to that of another, or any arrangements for
such a contingency as the possible death of
the king before the work was complete. On
the contrary, everything argues one continuous

---

beginning of a horizontal passage like that to the Queen's
Chamber, and finally the commencement of the upward rising
of the Grand Gallery with its remarkable ramps on either side.
The angles, heights, and breadths of all these are almost exactly
the same as obtain in the Great Pyramid." They are evidently
the experimental models, cut beforehand into an unneeded part
of the hill, giving the plan to which the Great Pyramid was
to be wrought, and to which the builders have accurately conformed the mighty structure. Here, then, in these trenches and
tubes we still find the plans and drawing to which these ancient
masons worked, both of the outside angles and the inside arrangements. We cannot conceive that these vast and still
enduring charts giving the features of the Great Pyramid in
all its greatness would thus have been cut if the whole work
had been conditioned to the uncertainty of the duration of the
king's life. Osburn entirely repudiates Lepsius's "law of
pyramid building."

and fore-calculated job, evenly carried through
from beginning to end, just as a farmer would
build his barn or a baker his oven.   Hence if
there is anything in Lepsius's " law of pyramid
building," the Great Pyramid never came
under it, but received its being and dimensions
from a foregoing plan of the whole, pursued
from commencement to completion without
interruption or any thought of it.

An immense amount of careful endeavor
has been expended by different men at different periods to ascertain the precise measurements of the Great Pyramid's base sides. And
since the discovery of the corner sockets it
would seem as if there should be no difficulty
in arriving at exact data on that point. But
the length to be measured is so great, and the
mounds of rubbish lying between the points
from which the measure is to be taken are so
immense and irregular, that absolute certainty
has not been reached and cannot be till some
rich man, society, or government performs the
work of removing the impediments and opens
a clear way from corner to corner. The
measurements thus far made from these sockets
by scientific men give us a mean of nine thousand one hundred and forty of our inches as
the length of either of the Great Pyramid's

four sides, that is, a fraction over seven hundred and sixty-one and a half feet, or nearly one-sixth of a mile.*

With this measure for the base of the sides, and the angle of 51° 51' 14" for their slope, the lines intersect in a point of perpendicular altitude five thousand eight hundred and nineteen inches from the level of the pavement discovered by Colonel Vyse. But there are other ways of ascertaining the height. By the barometer, by trigonometry, and by the actual measurement of the heights of the two hun-

---

* The following is a list of these measures:

The French savants in 1799, north side only, 9163 Eng. inches.
Colonel Howard Vyse in 1836, "   "   "   9168   "   "
Mahmoud Bey in 1862,   "   "   "   9162   "   "
Aiton and Inglis in 1865, mean of four sides, 9110   "   "
English Ordnance Surveyors in 1869, mean
    of four sides,   9130   "   "

Mean of the five,   9144   "   "

The Aiton-Inglis measuring was repeated four times, and the mean given is that of the four measures, which would justly entitle this figure to more weight than simply as one of the five. Very moderately weighting it beyond the rest gives us the general mean of nine thousand one hundred and forty inches, with a small margin of possible error on either side. It is greatly to be regretted that we cannot refer to absolutely certain figures, and so shut out all possible cavil; but as the matter stands, the most reasonable and scientific way of estimating the truth is that of taking the properly weighted mean of the several very competent measurers, each anxious to be exact, and one as liable to be too high as the other too low.

dred and two remaining courses of the masonry, the elevation to the present plateau at the top can be taken. And by eight of the most distinguished measurers who have performed the operation, from Jomard and Cecile to Aiton and Inglis, the mean comes out five thousand four hundred and forty inches. Prof. Smyth makes it five thousand four hundred and forty-five. Each side of the present summit area is four hundred inches. Adding one hundred inches, the thickness of the casing stones, to each side, the square would be six hundred inches on each outer line. At the angle of 51° 51' 14'' this would give a vertical height of three hundred and eighty-two inches, yielding $5440 + 382 = 5822$ of our inches as the full original height of the Great Pyramid. The same estimate is confirmed on other and independent methods of computation; thus also confirming the estimate of the length of the base sides, the one process yielding within three inches of what is reached by the other.

Within a narrow margin of uncertainty in which actual measurement always differs from absolute mathematical exactness, we may therefore take it as reasonably settled that the Great Pyramid's sides are each nine thousand one hundred and forty of our inches long, and slope upward to a point originally five thousand eight hundred and twenty of the same inches in perpendicular height above the line of the pavement below. This gives us the vastest and highest stone building ever erected by human hands.*

Osburn says, "its long shadow darkens the fields of Gizeh as the day declines," and that "when the spectator can obtain a distinct conception of its vastness no words can describe the overwhelming sense of it which rushes upon his mind. He feels oppressed and staggers beneath a load," to think that such a mountain was piled by the handiwork of man.

STANDARD OF LINEAR MEASURE.

From these measurements of size result the π proportion which is now admitted to be practically exhibited in this pyramid, whether

---

* The highest cathedrals in the world are Strasburg, five thousand six hundred and sixteen inches; Rouen, five thousand five hundred and sixty-eight; St. Stephen's, Vienna, five thousand two hundred and ninety-two; St. Peter's, Rome, five thousand one hundred and eighty-four; Amiens, five thousand and eighty-eight; Salisbury, four thousand eight hundred and forty-eight; Freiburg, four thousand six hundred and twenty; St. Paul's, London, four thousand three hundred and thirty-two. The Cathedral at Cologne was meant to be higher, but never has reached this height, neither has any other known tower. The oldest standing edifice in the world is thus the highest by far.

there by accident or by intention. The width is $\frac{\pi}{2}$ or $\frac{1}{7}$ of the height, and each face is almost exactly the square of the height.

From such high science we are also led to expect the record of some definite standard of measure, which every one would naturally wish to learn of from such wonderful architects and geometricians. Standards of measure are also just now a subject of special interest. There has come a singular disturbance and doubt on the part of legislators and *savants* as to what ought to be the ultimate reference or basis for all measures of length. The nations are inquiring, and nobody seems to know on what to rest. The French metres are unfortunately being urged by many as the most scientific known.

Nearly one hundred years ago the French people, in their first revolution, made an attempt to abolish alike the Christian religion and the hereditary weights and measures of all nations, seeking to supplant the former by a worship of philosophy and liberty, and the latter by a new scheme of metres. For their unit and standard of length they took the quadrant of the earth's surface at the particular meridian of Paris, divided it into ten million parts and so obtained the metre of 39.371 inches now

so highly eulogized. To say nothing of the
origin and motive of such a standard, the
science that is claimed for it is of no high
character.   It has the misfortune of taking a
curved line drawn on the earth's surface, and
that at a particular meridian no more fitting
than any other, instead of some straight line
invariable for all the earth.   Besides, in estimating for the earth's elliptic meridian at Paris
these atheistic *savants*, as now proven, miscalculated to the extent of one part in every five
thousand three hundred too little, and so on
their own basis their lauded unit of length is
not scientifically true.   Sir John Herschel
rightfully pronounces it "the newest and worst
measure in the world," and Beckett Denison
justly regards it as an "inconvenient, inaccu-
rate, and *unstridable* measure."   What men
need is a universal standard afforded by nature,
and serving alike for all mankind.   For such
a standard M. Callet, in 1795, in his book on
Logarithms, suggested the axis of the earth,
the even ten millionth to be taken as the
standard with which to compare all distances
and lengths.   It was a grand thought, far in
advance of all modern science on the subject.
The axis of the earth has every philosophic
and æsthetic reason in its favor as the great

terrestrial reference for all our linear measurements. It is a *straight line*, the only unvarying straight line which terrestrial nature affords, and the same for all localities and all time. It is the base line to which the earth itself is framed. And as remarked by Sir John Herschel, so long as the human mind continues human and retains a power of geometry, such a line will be held of far superior importance to any part or degree of a circumference. And if any *axis* is to be chosen on which to found a scientific unit, the nature of things gives an absolute and indefeasible preference to the *polar* axis. Now this is precisely the standard of reference for linear measure which the Great Pyramid places before us.

The polar diameter of the earth, according to the best science, is 500,500,000 of our inches, within so small a limit of possible error as to make but little difference in so multitudinous a subdivision. The British ordnance survey gives the results of two methods of computation, one of which makes it 500,428,296, and the other 500,522,904 of our inches, the former being considered as having the preponderance in weight. The mean of the two would therefore be close about five hundred millions five hundred thousand of our inches ; and this is what Beckett Denison in his *Astronomy* gives as the result of the most reliable modern calculations.

Taking the even five hundred millionth part of this, we would have 1.001 of our inches. Suppose, then, that we free this even division of the earth's polar diameter from all fractions, and call the five hundred millionth part of that axis *one inch*. We would thus have a low and convenient unit of length, about half a fine hair's breadth longer than our present inch. So complete and even a deduction from the polar axis of the whole earth would certainly be the grandest, the most rational, and the most natural *standard of length* to be found in or on our globe. Twenty-five of these inches, that is, 25.025 of our inches, would then serve for a cubit or longer standard, evenly deduced, which, multiplied by 10⁷, would tell the exact distance from the centre of the earth to either pole. It would be the ten millionth part of the semi-axis of the globe we inhabit. And what is more, it would be the exact *sacred cubit* which God himself gave to His people of old, and

by which He directed all the sacred construc-
tions and their appurtenances to be formed.*

And these sublime earth commensurating
standards of length are precisely the ones set
forth in the Great Pyramid. Whether the
practical working measure was in general the
Egypto-Babylonian cubit of about twenty to
twenty-one of our inches or any other makes
no difference. The evidences are clear that *a
cubit* of 25.025 of our inches, or one within a
very slight fraction of that length, and *an inch*
which is the five hundred millionth part of
the earth's polar diameter, were in the minds
of the architects, and meant by them to be
most significantly emphasized.

---

* Some have doubted whether the Jews, either before or after
the Exodus, ever had a special cubit of this kind. But that
they had, and that the same was a Divinely given and author-
ized length measure, is so clearly deducible from the Scriptures
and the Jewish writings in general that there ought to be no
question about it.   Sir Isaac Newton, in his " Dissertation on
Cubits," has brought this out so conclusively as to leave but little
else to be desired. By five successive methods he also deduces
the limit of its length as in no case less than 23.3 or more than
27.9 of our inches. The mean of all his numbers amounts to
25.07 of our inches, with a possible error on the one side or the
other of one-tenth of an inch. That the Hebrews, then, had a
peculiar and sacred cubit wholly separate from all other cubits,
and that it was the even ten millionth part of the semi-axis of
the earth, we may accept and hold on the authority of one of
the greatest minds and one of the most thorough and competent investigators of such a matter that has illuminated our
modern times.

It is a noble and fitting thought that as the existence of an axis of rotation in the earth *makes* the days, the grand standard of length founded on that axis should *count* them. And so it is in the Great Pyramid. This nature-derived cubit is contained in each side of this edifice just as many times as there are days in a year! This simple fact is of itself an invincible demonstration that these builders had such a length in mind as their greatest and most sacred standard and enumerator of linear measure. But it is also specially singled out and recorded elsewhere in the edifice. It is the top width of the grand niche in the Queen's Chamber, and the distance between the highest inner edge of that niche and the vertical centre of the chamber. It is thus set before the eye as if to teach all to note its existence and to search for its hidden use and meaning in the symbolizations.

As to the inch or the one-twenty-fifth of this measure, being an integer of the grand day counter, it, too, is indicated in the right place and in the right way. It is contained separately and independently in the entire perimeter of the Grand Pyramid's base, just one hundred times for each day of the year. As the low unit of count in measure, it is also the representative of a year in the reckoning of the passage floor-lines as charts of history, as also in the diagonals of the pyramid's base taken as a measure of the precessional cycle. It is likewise specially exhibited in connection with the cubit in the singular boss of the suspended "granite leaf" in the anteroom to the King's Chamber.*   Besides, when multiplied by 10^{7+4} it serves to tell in round decimals the distance through space which the earth travels in each complete revolution on its axis, that is 100,000,000,000 inches.

A standard of length measure is thus exhibited which fits with grand evenness to nature in her great facts, but no less beautifully with what is common and homely. We used to be taught that the inch is made up of so many

---

* Captain Tracy has pointed out that the pyramid's earth-commensurated cubit is exhibited on this *boss* of the granite leaf divided into fives, for it is just one-fifth of that cubit broad, and the thickness of the *boss* is again just one-fifth of its width. We thus have the earth-commensurated *inch* and *cubit* exhibited together, five times five of the one constituting the other. This *boss* again is just one of these inches aside from the centre of the block on which it is, and the distance from its centre to the eastern end of that block in its groove is just one cubit of twenty-five of these inches.   Rev. Glover re-examined the measures of this *boss* in 1874 and says: " I find it most fairly confirmatory of the entire of the sacred cubit and its divisions, giving the inch elevation and the five-inch span with an inch base for the side slope ; on the boss itself there is no indication whatever of any irregularity of shape."—CASEY's " Philitis," p. 40.

barleycorns. That reference, I believe, has been expunged from our arithmetic tables, because our mathematicians have lost the knowledge and meaning of our hereditary unit of length. But such is the fact, which any one can test for himself, that if we start with the average length of the grains from which man gets his bread, or with the average breadth of a man's thumb, length of arm, or reach of step in easy walking, everything comes out closely even with these earth commensurated and Divinely approved standards of length, and with these alone.

WEIGHT AND CAPACITY MEASURE.

And as these great old architects *measured* the earth, so they also *weighed* it. As nearly as can be computed, their pyramid is the even one thousand billionth part of the weight of this whole earth-ball of land and sea. The gravity of the entire mass of what they built needs only to be multiplied by $10^{5 \times 3}$ to indicate the sum of the gravity of the entire mass of the globe we inhabit.

There has been much effort expended by modern science to find out the mean density or specific gravity of the earth, without exactly settling the problem. The best experiments make it between 5.316 and 6.565 times the weight of water at the medium temperature of 68° Fahrenheit. The Great Pyramid makes it 5.70, which is almost exactly the mean of the best five experiments ever made.*

A further memorial of the same is furnished in the Coffer of the King's Chamber, in whose structure the same π proportions of the pyramid itself reappear in another form. The

---

* These experiments as given in "Johnson's New Universal Cyclopædia" (Art. Density of the Earth), are the following:

Colonel James's Observations with Arthur's Seat, .	5.316
Prof. Airy's Mine Experiments, ...	6.565
Cavendish Leaden Globe Experiment, . . .	5.480
Reich's Experiments, ...	5.438
Baily's Experiments, ...	5.660
Mean of all the results, ...	5.672
Difference from pyramid, ...	.028
Pyramid expression, ...	5.700

It thus appears that the pyramid's figure for the earth's density is much nearer to the mean of the experiments than the experiments are to each other.

Computing the earth's bulk at a mean gravity 5.7 times that of water, according to the calculation made by Mr. Wm. Petrie, of London, the figures stand thus:

Pyramid's mass in tons, 5,272,600.
Earth's mass in tons,   5,271,900,000,000,000,000,000.

The accurate calculation of such immense masses of matter must necessarily be very rough; but the results come out evenly enough to show that 5.70 is the proper figure for the pyramidic estimate of the mean density of the earth, and that the pyramid was meant to be of such weight that it should be to the whole weight of the earth as 1 to $10^{5 \times 3}$.

internal capacity of that Coffer by the nicest possible computations is seventy-one thousand two hundred and fifty cubic pyramid or earth-commensurated inches. The only intelligible reason for that particular *capacity* is to be found in the combination of a capacity and weight measure standard, having reference to the size and gravity of the earth, with that gravity computed at 5.7. Even the long-unobserved little irregularities of that Coffer come in as a necessary modifying element to meet precisely the earth reference formula. On the pyramid system of *fives*, 50^3 earth-commensurated inches multiplied by the earth's specific gravity and divided by 10, represent with close exactness the Coffer's interior space.

To the reality of these earth references at the valuations given, this Coffer comes in as a seal, and at the same time furnishes a grand standard of united weight and capacity measure. At the rate of 5.7 for the mean density of the earth, the Coffer's contents of water at 68° Fahrenheit would be equal to twelve thousand five hundred cubic inches of the body of the earth. Dividing this into two thousand five hundred equal parts for a small fraction in the dominant pyramid number we have an even result equal to five cubic inches of the earth's mean density, which would be the pyramid or earth-commensurated *pound*, which is, within a small fraction, the same as *our common avoirdupois pound*, equal in weight to a pint, 5 × 5.7 cubic inches of water at a temperature of 68° Fahrenheit.

THE COFFER AND THE ARK OF THE COVENANT.

The only article of furniture in all the Great Pyramid is this Coffer in the King's Chamber. Al Mamoun found it a lidless, empty box, cut from a solid block of red granite, and polished within and without. In shape it is an oblong rectangular trough, without inscription or ornament, and of such size that it could not possibly have been taken in or out of its place since the pyramid was built. Its proportions are all geometrical. Its sides and bottom are cubically identical with its internal space. The length of its two sides to its height is as a circle to its diameter. Its exterior volume is just twice the dimensions of its bottom, and its whole measure is just the fiftieth part of the size of the chamber in which it stands. Its internal space is just four times the measure of an English " quarter" of wheat. By its contents measure it also confirms Sir Isaac Newton's determination of the length of the

sacred cubit of twenty-five earth-commensurated inches. The holy Ark of the Tabernacle
and the Temple, according to the Scriptures,
was two and a half cubits long, and one and
a half broad and high. This must be outside
measure, as the records speak of *height* and not
of *depth*. With twenty-five earth-commensurated inches to a cubit, and allowing 1.8 of
these inches for the thickness of the boards,
its internal space would be seventy-one thousand two hundred and eighty-two of the same
cubic inches, or within thirty-two of the number of such cubic inches in the capacity measure of the pyramid Coffer. Or allowing 1.75
inches for the thickness of the sides and ends
and two inches for the bottom, the inner cubical
contents would be seventy-one thousand two
hundred and thirteen inches, or within thirty-
seven of the Coffer. The mean of these two
estimates, which must include all reasonable
suppositions for the carpentry of the ark,
would be seventy-one thousand two hundred
and forty-eight cubic inches, which is within
two inches of the best computation of the internal dimensions of the pyramid Coffer. That
they should be thus alike in internal measure,
the dimensions of the one having been specially laid down by God himself, is very remark-

able, and that the two should thus mutually
sustain each other in the recognition of one and
the same earth-commensurated cubit, is both
striking and significant.   Nay, using this same
earth-commensurated cubit as identical with
the sacred cubit, the further result appears
that the Jewish laver and the Ark of the
Tabernacle were the same in capacity measure
with the pyramid's Coffer, and that Solomon's
molten sea was just fifty times the capacity
of either of these and exactly equal in interior
cubic space with the King's Chamber itself.

TEMPERATURE.

As the Great Pyramid stands on the line
which equally divides the surface of the northern hemisphere, there is at once a close
approach of its climate to the mean temperature of all the earth's surface, at least of every
habitable land and navigable sea.   According
to the French *savants*, by observations both in
and outside of the Great Pyramid, that temperature is about 68° Fahrenheit.   A permanent
and unvarying record of this temperature is
maintained in the pyramid's granite chamber,
which is so buried in masonry as not to be
affected by external changes, and furnished with
a system of ventilating tubes to keep every-

thing exactly normal within. This degree of temperature is exactly one-fifth of the distance which mercury rises in the tube between the freezing and boiling-points of water, and furnishes the basis for a complete nature-adjusted pyramid system of thermal measure. Dividing this one-fifth by the standard of fifty (the room in which the index of temperature is arranged being the chamber of fifty), we have the even two hundred and fifty for the degrees between the two notable points of nature marked by the freezing and boiling of common water. Multiplying this by four, say the pyramid's four sides, we are brought to another great natural heat-mark, namely, that at which heat begins to give forth light, and iron, the commonest of metals, becomes red. Then multiplying again by five, say by the number of the pyramid's five corners, the result comes out evenly at another grand nature-marked point of thermal measure, namely, that at which heat shows whiteness, and platinum, the densest and most refractory of metals, melts.

A Metrological Monument.

Thus the Great Pyramid proves itself abundantly competent to determine on a natural and most scientific basis all measures of length, weight, capacity, and heat. Even the degrees in the circle if arranged on the pyramid numbers, say one thousand degrees instead of the fractional Babylonian three hundred and sixty, some think, would be vastly more natural and easy than it is. This would divide the quadrant into the convenient two hundred and fifty with even tenths for minutes and seconds, whilst it would at the same time harmoniously commensurate with navigation and itinerary measures of knots and miles, into which it is now so troublesome to translate from the indications of the sextant.

There would seem, therefore, to be nothing wanting in this mighty monument of hoar antiquity for the formation of a metrical system the most universal in its scope, the most scientifically founded in its standards, the most happily interrelated, and the most easy in its common use that ever was presented to the contemplation of man or that can be employed for our earth purposes. And it is devoutly to be wished, if the present agitation of the human mind with regard to standards and systems of measure is to result in any changes for the nations, that they should be in the line of what Providence has thus set before mankind. Great Britain, the United States,

the German Empire, the Scandinavian King-
doms, and other principalities and countries,
have this system already almost exact in some
departments, descended to them they know
not from whence, and the correction of what
is faulty would be attended with infinitely less
discomfort than the introduction of French
metrès, conceived in rebellion against the
common faith and order of the Christian world.
We would then have the high consciousness of
possessing a system of metrology the most
ancient and the most self-consistent in the
world, and one in most profound accord with
nature as God made it, if not communicated
by the great God of nature by direct inspiration from His eternal wisdom.*

---

* We subjoin a table of units and standards of this system
the better to set it before the eyes and understandings of those
disposed to investigate its elements.

I. LINEAR MEASURE. The grand standard for this is the
earth's axis of rotation, the sacred cubit of Noah, Moses, Solomon, and the Great Pyramid, the shortest distance from the
centre of the earth to either pole divided by 10⁷, which is equal
to 25.025 of our inches. The table would then run as follows:

3 barleycorns	= 1 inch or thumb-breadth.
25 inches	= 1 cubit, arm-length, or pace.
100 cubits	= 1 acre side.
25 acre sides	= 1 mile.
4 miles	= 1 league.

II. WEIGHT AND CAPACITY MEASURE. The grand standard for this is the mean density of the earth at 5.70 times the

THE PYRAMID'S ASTRONOMY.

Nor are we any less impressed with the singular wonderfulness of this ancient pillar, when we come to look more directly at its astronomy.

Figuring the framework of the earth as a triangle formed from a line of diameter, and referring to an axis for a basis for this triangle as well as a grand standard of measure, and that triangle being greater in vertical height by

---

weight of water at 68° Fahrenheit, weighing five cubic inches to the pound, which is 1.028 of the pound avoirdupois, or 1.050 old French " poids de marc," or one pint, 5 × 5.70 cubic inches of water 68° Fahrenheit (50° pyramid), barometrical pressure thirty inches of preceding table, dividing downward by ten and twenty for ounces, drachms, and grains, and multiplying upwards by ten for a stone, ten again for hundredweight, then by five for a quarter, and then by four for the ton, and the same for gallons, bushels, quarters, and chaldrons.

The interrelations would then be:

1 drop of water	= 1 grain.
1 pint	= 1 pound.
1 bushel	= 1 hundredweight.
1 chaldron	= 1 ton.

III. THERMAL MEASURE. The grand standard for this is the mean temperature of the earth in which man works with most ease and comfort, 68° Fahrenheit, 20° Centigrade.

0, zero, the freezing-point of water.
50, mean temperature of the whole earth.
250, boiling-point of water.
1000, the point at which heat reddens iron.
5000, white heat, at which platinum melts.

duplication than would equal the width of its base, the earth is necessarily contemplated as a spheroid—a globe thicker at the equator than at the poles—just as all correct astronomy now represents it. Modern science ascribes the discovery of this spherity of the earth to Thales, six hundred years before Christ; but here it is more perfectly represented than Thales ever knew, more than fifteen hundred years before Thales was born.

A fixed axis would also seem to imply the idea of rotatory motion. And the making of the sides of the pyramid to record an even fraction of the earth's axis of rotation just as many times as there are days in the year, proves that these builders had an idea of both motions of the earth, and a knowledge of the number of times it revolves on its own axis in making its annual revolution around the sun. This latter motion they also further symbolized by the inches or fractions of twenty-five in their great standard of length, just one hundred of which to a day, for the number of days in the year, are contained in the perimeter of the pyramid's base. If any one within historic times prior to Copernicus and Galileo really understood this feature of our globe, it certainly was not well known nor much believed till after these men had lived ; and yet, here it is distinctly and truly symbolized more than thirty-five hundred years before their time.

These ancient architects also knew where to find the poles of the earth, since they were able to determine latitude and what degree of latitude marks the half-way of the world's surface between the equator and the poles. This they prove to us by having built their pyramid on that line of latitude, namely, on the thirtieth north. It is, in fact, a slight fraction south of that line as now estimated, but obviously intended to indicate that degree, since they built as closely to the northern brink of the hill as it was possible to go and yet secure a permanent foundation for their work. Nor is it much further from that line than the ranges of probable error in the best scientific calculations. By three distinct processes (by differences of zenith distance, by absolute zenith distances, and by transits in prime verticle) lately made to determine precisely the latitude of Mt. Agamenticus Station in Maine, each differed from the others, and the determination could not be made any nearer than somewhere within the fourth of a hundred parts of a second. This was close enough for all practical purposes, but shows that the best science cannot be precisely exact on the subject. And yet, here we have a determination made more than four thousand years ago, in fact almost within the limit of error of the best scientific possibilities, and with the plain intimation of a better knowledge which had to be sacrificed to the requirements for a fitting basis to a building intended to last to the end of time.

These men have thus left us the memorial of a remarkable geodesy, which is further exhibited in the fact that they not only put their pillar in the very centre of Egypt, but on the pivotal balance-point of the entire land distribution over the face of the whole earth. A glance at any universal map makes this apparent, whilst we look in vain for another point on all the globe which so naturally and evenly marks the centre of equation for all inhabited land surface. There is here a measurement or consciousness of the extent and proportional relations and distribution of the earth's continents and islands, such as modern science has not yet furnished or even attempted to give.

There is perhaps no much better test of a sound, practical astronomy, than to be able to determine truly the four cardinal points. A very simple and easy thing most persons would think it, but not so easy when brought to the test. The compass alone never can be depended on, except in a general way. The attempts of men to orient truly, even with the aid of science, have shown constant inaccuracy. It used to be thought a great matter to have churches and cathedrals built exactly east and west; but of all so intended scarcely one has been found that does not incline either to the north or the south of the line meant to be followed. It is the same even with buildings erected specially for astronomical purpose. Tycho Brahe's celebrated Uranibourg observatory is faulty in orientation to five minutes of a degree. The Greeks in the height of their glory could not find the cardinal points astronomically within eight degrees. But the builders of the Great Pyramid, out in the Lybian desert, with no guide or landmark but the naked stars, were able to orient their structure so exactly that the science of the wisest Athenian sages, eighteen hundred years afterwards, was seventy times, and the observatory of Uranibourg nearly four times, further out of the way than it is.

One of the most curious and important problems of astronomy is the sun distance, at which men have labored so long and so earnestly without being able to solve it closer than within a limit of error embracing a million and a half of miles. That distance, however, is emphatically and definitely pronounced in the Great Pyramid, by its 10 and 9 of practical erection, as the even 10^9 times its own height, which is about the mean between the highest and lowest figures which the most recent observations have set down as the best results science has reached on this point.

THE PYRAMID'S CHRONOLOGY.

Time reckonings belong to the same subject. Things can have no place or being without *time*. And as measures of time are mere notations of motions in the clockwork of the universe, chronology and astronomy necessarily go together. And as the Great Pyramid memorializes the one, the other must also be embraced. Memorializing the revolutions of the earth on its own axis and around the sun, it thus at the same time fixes its notation of days and the year.

But there is another observable movement going on in the universe of a much grander and wider range, and of special importance with regard to chronology. It forms a sacred clock, whose face is the sky, and from which we may read backwards or forwards for thousands on thousands of years without the possibility of confusion, the same as we read the hours and minutes on a timepiece. It is what astronomers call " the precession of the equinoxes."

There is a twofold year, one called the siderial year, or year of the stars, and the other the year of the sun or seasons, the equinoctial year. The former is a fraction longer than the latter. That is to say, the equinoxes in our ordinary practical year come a little earlier every time than the siderial time. This precedence in the equinoctial presentations amounts to about fifty seconds each year, and is hence called the precession of the equinoxes. It is really a retardation in the time of the rising and setting of the stars, by which they come about fifty seconds later every year. It was Hipparchus, about one hundred and fifty years before Christ, who first noted this within historic times; and since his day the rising and setting of the stars, as compared with the equinoctial or common year, has fallen back about thirty degrees from what their time then was. At this rate of retardation it takes about nine and a half millions of our days or about twenty-five thousand eight hundred and sixty-eight of our years for this rising and setting to come back again to the exact point at which we begin the calculation. We thus have a great astronomical cycle, less than a fourth of which has passed since man was placed upon the earth. It furnishes a singularly valuable means of noting and determining remote dates. Knowing the relative places of the stars which most plainly mark this cycle, we can tell exactly how they stood in any year or date since time began; and knowing how they stood at the time of any given event, we can thus calculate the precise year almost to the day and hour in which that event took place.

Now if the Great Pyramid was meant to give us a symbolization of the physical universe, this grand year could not be overlooked, though science has been so long in finding it out. Nor has it been overlooked. It is all here plainly enough to be traced, just at the place and in the forms which we might expect. It is the greatest of nature's time-cycles, and its years would naturally be signified in the pyramid's lowest units of measure in the longest lines within the circle of its perimeter on which we read the days and years. The two diagonals of the Great Pyramid's base, taken together, measure just as many inches as this cycle has years.*

It has only been since the times of Tycho Brahe that astronomers began to have any assurance in determining the length of this period. The latest and closest calculations by Bessel make it twenty-five thousand eight hundred and sixty-eight years, which is the sum of inches in the diagonal measures of this pyramid's base, more accurately given than it was known when Newton and Hutton wrote. It has been thought to weaken the idea of intention on the part of the architects thus to symbolize this cycle, since the measure of the diagonals is necessarily resultant from the lengths of the sides. But this interdepend- ence of the diagonals and square in the pyramid's count of days, years, and the grand cycle of years, only proves that God has so constituted the motions of the heavenly bodies that a correct symbolization of one true count of nature involves the other, and that the

---

* A singular coincidence with this has been pointed out by R. A. Procter. If we take the pyramid's cubits instead of its inches, and multiply the number of these cubits in a base side of the pyramid by the number fifty, and increase the result in proportion as the base diagonal exceeds the measure of the side, the sum comes out in the number of years in the great preces- sional period.

mind which governed in the framing of the symbol was conscious of the fact.

It is by means of this cycle, in connection with its star-pointings, that the Great Pyramid also tells the date of its erection. Sir John Herschel in 1839, assuming that its long, narrow, polished tubular entrance passage was meant to be levelled at a polar star, began to calculate back with what data he had to find the time when such a star was looking down that tube from the northern heavens. Nor did he fail to find one answering the conditions near about the time assigned by other methods as the probable date at which the Great Pyramid was built. Closer determinations of the exact pointings of the grand tube, along with other data, enabled other astronomers to repeat the calculation with more determinate results, fixing upon the year two thousand one hundred and seventy before Christ, as that in which this tube pointed to α Draconis, the then pole star, at its lower culmination, at the same time that the Pleiades, particularly Alcyone, the centre of the group, were on the same meridian above. And as this was a mark in the heavens which could not occur again for more than twenty-five thousand years from that time, and was itself very extraordinary, it has been accepted as meant to be the sign of the date of the building of the Great Pyramid.

But what is thus astronomically made out is surprisingly corroborated in another way. These low tubular passage-ways prove themselves to be time charts also. They symbolize scrolls of human history as well as point out stars, and the notations in the one answer exactly to the other. The inch as a unit for a year also appears in these avenues. The entrance tube begins a record with the dispersion after the flood, and dates from the formation of nations. The history is a downward one under a dragon star toward a bottomless pit. Following this decline for about one thousand inches, which denote years, we reach the first upward passage. At that date the children of Israel, by special interposition of God, began their national economy and history. Following this ascending passage fifteen hundred and forty-two inches, the number of years from the Exodus of Israel to the birth of Christ, the last inch brings us to the beginning of the Grand Gallery, which sublimely symbolizes our Christian dispensation. Counting back, then, from the beginning of this gallery, that is, from the birth of Christ, 1542 inches to the entrance passage, and then up the entrance passage 628 inches more (1542 + 628 making 2170, the astronomical date of the pyramid's building), at the precise point we find a distinct and beautifully cut line ruled into the stone sides of the passage from top to bottom, put there by the builders of the edifice.*

And that these lines were meant to mark the time of the Great Pyramid's erection, the indication is distinctly given. The joinings of the stones of which the sides of this passage are built are all at right angles with its incline, except in two instances. The exceptions are the first two joints preceding these lines.

---

* The existence of these lines, as first reported by Prof. Smyth, has now been amply verified. Rev. F. R. A. Glover, on his way to India, in 1874, visited the Great Pyramid with some four or five others, and subsequently wrote from Cairo, under date of November 12th, " One of our party having quoted the opinion expressed by Sir Nelson Pycroft, ' that the story of these lines was all bosh,' I took care to let the party have ocular demonstration of their existence, and thus see the folly of the honorable baronet in declaring that ' these lines were not there, whatever Prof Smyth or anybody else had said.' When I had showed the young gentlemen above named that the lines were there, I said to them, ' Now you see that however difficult it may be to distinguish them by superficial observers, *the lines are there*, and I shall ask you to confess now, and at all other times, that *you have seen them*.' To this they gladly consented; and so this story and this verification of *the reality of the lines* will be repeated as often as I shall be called on to speak of the matter."—Given in Casey's " Philitis," pp. 40, 41.

These, instead of being at right angles with
the passage, are *vertical*, a figure of speech in
stone plainly indicative of lifting up or building.   And immediately after this signifying of
the process of erection, comes these thin, fine,
and beautiful lines, just two thousand one hundred and seventy inches from the beginning
of the Grand Gallery, which, as the beginning
of our dispensation would be the time of
Christ's birth.

Thus, then, by a double method, each equally
verifiable and distinct, and the one answering
exactly to the other, the Great Pyramid tells
its own age in time-marks as unmistakable as
they are true to the mysteries of the sky and
to the succession of events and dispensations
on the earth.

And in the same way this remarkable pillar
seems also to indicate the true date of the
flood.   If we count back from the date of its
erection six hundred and thirty years, and
inquire into the star-markings with regard to
the precessional cycle at that period, we find
the same pole star *a* Draconis looking down
that same entrance passage as at the time of
the building, but then *Aquarius*, the waterman,
instead of the Pleiades is on the meridian above,
the line crossing the very mouth of the vessel

whence the mighty stream is issuing. This could hardly have been without the knowledge of the designer of this edifice, and presents a very grand and remarkable time-mark. Can any one fail to have suggested to him what it indicates? All nations have preserved the tradition of it. The Scriptures refer to it again and again in the Old Testament and in the New. And the names and pictures of the constellations, as they still stand in our almanacs, unalterably point back to it. It is the great deluge of Noah's time, which the Great Pyramid thus locates chronologically at a point within a few years of the mean of the dates given for that event in the two different versions of the Scriptures, the Hebrew and the Septuagint, to wit, two thousand eight hundred years before Christ, and six hundred and thirty years before the building of the pyramid itself.

Septenaries and Sabbaths.

But time reckonings demand some special system of smaller fractions which cannot be made by mere decades, tens, or hundreds. The year and the day are such distinct and emphatic units of nature that man is compelled to observe them in his notations, and they will

not subdivide or multiply into each other by
even decimals. The French *savants* tried it,
but utterly failed, and after all their efforts
were compelled to fall back upon the old week
of seven days, which God himself ordained
from the beginning of the world as the easiest
and most practical system of ordinary time
commensuration. We would therefore expect
the Great Pyramid as a great symbol of nature
to have some reference to this also. And in
spite of its intense *fiveness*, it does not fail to
present this easier and sacredly approved division of days into weeks of sevens. Having
made so grand a reference to the Pleiades, or
the *seven stars*, the elemental grouping of
sevens at once comes in. Hence, the Grand
Gallery is seven times the average height of
the other passages, and its sides are built of
seven overlapping stone courses on either side.
So the passage which leads under it to the so-
called Queen's Chamber has a section distinctly
though differently marked off at its ends,
either of which is the one-seventh of that
passage's entire length. A septenary system
is thus recognized and indicated.

But it is not simply septenary, but likewise
sabbatic, at least as respects the Queen's Chamber and the way to it. There is a seventh

marked off from the six, and specially emphasized. The last seventh of the horizontal way
to that chamber is deeply indented in the floor,
so as to make the passage there about one-third
higher than anywhere else. This alone would
be decisive. But the chamber thus approached
through a sabbatic avenue is itself the culmination of a sabbatic system. By reason of its
peaked and two-sided ceiling it is a seven-
sided room; and the amount of cubic space
thus divided off above the square at the top
is the high seventh of the cubic space contained above the distinctly marked base line
which runs around the room at the height
of the passage conducting into it. It is thus
a completed sabbatism founded on a sabbatism
in the way by which it is approached. We
thus have all the features of the Hebrew sabbatic system emphatically pronounced and
most remarkably built into the rocky structure
of this pyramid more than six hundred years
before Moses and the giving of the law,—a
system of which the Gentiles as such knew
little or nothing, though practically observed
by the Creator himself in the great week in
which the world was made. And by this
intense sabbatism we are doubtless to identify
this part of the pyramid with the Jew, the

same as we identify the Grand Gallery with the Christian dispensation.

THE CENTRE OF THE UNIVERSE.

But there is a yet grander thought embodied in this wonderful structure. Of its five points, there is one of special pre-eminence, in which all its sides and upward exterior lines terminate. It is the summit corner, which lifts its solemn index-finger to the sun at midday, and by its distance from the base tells the mean distance of that sun from the earth. And if we go back to the date which the pyramid gives itself, and look for what that finger pointed to at midnight, we find a far sublimer indication.

Science has at last discovered that the sun is not a dead centre, with planets and comets wheeling about it but itself stationary. It is now ascertained that the sun also is in motion, carrying with it its splendid retinue of comets, planets, its satellites and theirs, around some other and vastly mightier centre. Astronomers are not yet fully agreed as to what or where that centre is. Some, however, believe that they have found the direction of it to be the Pleiades, and particularly *Alcyone*, the central one of the renowned Pleiadic stars. To the distinguished German astronomer, Prof. J. H.

Maedler, belongs the honor of having made this discovery. Alcyone, then, as far as science has been able to perceive, would seem to be " the midnight throne " in which the whole system of gravitation has its central seat, and from which the Almighty governs His universe. And here is the wonderful corresponding fact, that at the date of the Great Pyramid's completion, at midnight of the autumnal equinox, and hence the true beginning of the year as still preserved in the traditions of many nations, the Pleiades were distributed over the meridian of this pyramid, with *Alcyone* (η Tauri) precisely on the line.

Here, then, is a pointing of the highest and sublimest character that mere human science has ever been able so much as to hint, and which would seem to breathe an unsuspected and mighty meaning into that speech of God to Job when He demanded, " *Canst thou bind the sweet influences of Pleiades ?*"

WHENCE THIS WISDOM?

Could all these things have been mere coincidences? Is it possible that they just happened so out of blind chance? Then what is the reason that nothing of the sort has happened in the scores of other Egyptian pyramids?

And if they were really designed by the builders, whence then came this surprising intelligence, unsurpassed and uncontradictable by the best scientific attainments of modern man ?

Shall we credit it all to old Egypt? We find it memorialized *in* Egypt, but could it have been *of* Egypt? Not far can we go in such an inquiry till we find the way impassably choked up against any such conclusion. The old Egyptians never were a highly scientific people. Bunsen says, " Their astronomy was strictly provincial, calculated only for the meridian of Egypt ;" and that " the signs of the zodiac were wholly unknown to them till the reign of Trajan." Brugsch says, " It was based on empiricism, and not on that mathematical science which calculates the movements of the stars." Strabo admits that the Egyptians of his day were destitute of scientific astronomical knowledge. Renan asserts, and Edward Everett had said before him, that " Not a reformer, not a great poet, not a great artist, not a *savant*, not a philosopher, is to be met with in all their history." Never, therefore, was it in their power to understand, much less originate and enunciate, the sublime science found in the Great Pyramid. The other pyramids were *of* Egypt, but they are totally wanting in all these elements of intellectuality. We look in vain for any traces that the old Egyptians ever understood the mathematical π, much less construct so original a symbol of it. There is no proof that they ever had any appreciation of the pyramid's system of numbers, or knew anything of the sun's distance or the earth's form or weight. There is no sign that they ever used the pyramid inch, or the cubit of twenty-five inches, or any measure founded on intelligent earth commensuration. There is nothing to show that they comprehended the precessional cycle, or ever made use of it. They computed by the short and confusing Sothic cycle of one thousand four hundred and sixty-one years, and mistook even that, making it a day in every four years shorter than it really is. Their governing star was not Alcyone, the happy star of celestial tranquillity and peace, but *Sirius*, the fiery dogstar, whose rising and setting with the sun marks " the dog days,"—the most pestilential days of all the year. It is a bright and flaring star, indeed, but of ill omen to the northern and more classic peoples—a star of which Homer sung as one

Whose burning breath
Taints the red air with fevers, plagues, and death.

—a star fittingly auspicious of the beast worship
of the people who regulated their grand cycle
by it. And when we further consider how
perfectly clear and pure the Great Pyramid is
from all marks or traces of old Egypt's super-
abounding idolatry, which " changed the glory
of the uncorruptible God into an image made
like to corruptible man, and to birds, and four-
footed beasts, and creeping things," defiling
every object with this base harlotry of the
human soul; it becomes utterly impossible to
believe that this grand pillar, with its still
grander scientific embodiments, could ever
have sprung from Egypt, though "all the
wisdom of the Egyptians " had been concen-
trated to produce it. Many pyramids did
Egypt build before the costly fashion went out
of vogue; but even with the great original
before them, there was not genius and observation enough in all the land to make so much
as a correct copy of it. Of all the enormous
mounds of brick or stone which Egypt itself
set up, there is not one to tell of aught but
vaulting ambition and blundering imitation.
From the least unto the greatest there is
neither science nor sense in any of them.
How then could Egypt have originated this
great science-laden forerunner of them all?

Whence then came this wisdom? Some direct us to Babylon as the fountain-head of science and astronomy. And the Chaldæans were, indeed, great builders and astrologers. They worshipped the heavenly bodies. Among them, if among any of the nations, may we best hope to find the primal treasure-house of the knowledge we have been deciphering, if it be at all of earth. To the planet temple of Nebo, at Borsippa, are we above all directed as the best memorial they have left us. But the Borsippa temple comes seventeen hundred years after the Great Pyramid, and yet sinks into insignificance beside it. Its orientation has been specially lauded as strikingly scientific for that remote age, and yet its builders missed it by six degrees! And so lopsided was that construction according to the best reproductions of its plan,—its surface so broken with corners of terraces, panelled walls, priests' dwellings, and flights of steps, that its warmest admirers do not pretend to find anything scientific in its form or shape. It was dedicated to the planets, and proposed to enumerate them in its diverse colored stages, and yet it knew nothing of Uranus, Neptune, or the planetoids, and counted in the earth's moon as one! With such an astronomy the

Great Pyramid could not possibly have been made what it is. There is, indeed, a system of Babylonian metres which has penetrated more or less into all civilized countries, principally through Alexander and the Greeks; but it was a system of *sixes* and *sevens*, and not of *fives* and *tens*. Its cubit was between twenty and twenty-one inches, and not the twenty-five of the earth-commensurated cubit of the Great Pyramid and the sacred cubit of the Hebrews. And no more in Babylon's metrology than in Babylon's planet temple is there any real science worthy of the name. There is *measure*, but it is meaningless. There is grand *building*, but it is only fanciful piling up of bricks and stories which tells of nothing but the pride and idolatry of the builders and their blundering in the plain things of our planetary economy, beyond which there is nothing. Never from such a source could the Great Pyramid have come.

Whence, then, came this wisdom? Step by step we are being driven to the border line of the territory of miracle and inspiration. Nor do I know how we can honestly help ourselves against crossing it for an explanation. Prof. Proctor has recently undertaken to solve the whole matter on very easy human grounds,

but the flippancy with which he disposes of
some of the problems, while taking no account
whatever of others, shows that, astronomer as
he is, he has not fully taken in the case. The
whole thing bears the impress of an intelligence so high, a wisdom so unaccountable, and
a beneficence so genial toward the wants of
man, that no one yet has even begun to show
how it can be less than supernatural. And
yet our presentations have followed but one
line of inquiry, while there are others of still
more striking character and importance. I
have kept myself thus far to the department
of science alone. But there remain sundry
other fields full of wonder, on which I have
not time now to touch.

Six hundred years had this pyramid been
built before Moses began to write the Penta-
teuch. And what if passages should be found
scattered through the Scriptures which will
not intelligibly interpret without it? What
if all the great doctrines of Revelation, and all
the great characteristics of the ages, and all
the mightiest facts in human history and God's
administrations, should be found imbedded in
its rocky symbolisms? What if we should
find it prophesied of as a grand memorial of
Jehovah, meant to be uncovered and read in

these last evil times, in confutation of the degrading philosophies and vain conceits which
men untaught of God would have us accept
in place of the word of Revelation? What
if we should hear from out its dark and long-
hidden chambers and avenues just where we
are in the great calendar of time, what scenes
are next to be expected in the affairs of our
world and what unexampled changes presently
await us? What if it should turn out to be a
clear and manifest prophecy of man's constant
native deterioration, of his redemption by
miracle, and of his destiny forever, all written
out beforehand in "the grandeur of immortal
stone?" What if it should prove itself an
earlier and independent duplicate of God's
volume of inspiration? What majesty and
consequence would it then assume in the eyes
of all right-thinking men! To what a crushing test would our modern scientists then be
brought with their theories of creation without a God and their doctrines of salvation
without a Saviour!

Nor is it an extravagant anticipation to expect even thus much from this wonderful
pillar. Once admit, as I believe it will yet
have to be admitted, that superhuman intelligence is in it, and there is then every reason

to count on finding the whole story. God never deals in fragments without making them symbols of the whole. And I shall be much mistaken if it does not turn out, without forcing of facts or dealing in fancies, that in these rocks and their emplacements are treasured up from hoar antiquity the whole plan of God in grace and miracle as well as in the universe of nature. Some other opportunity may be afforded for us to enter and survey this field and thus penetrate further into this glorious mountain of glorious thoughts.

Meanwhile, the mighty structure stands immortal in its greatness, lifting its brow the nearest to heaven of all earthly works, and asserting in every feature something more than human. With all of man's workmanship that went before it in utter ruin, it stands only the more readable from the damages of time, the grand and indestructible monument of the true primeval man. Upon its pedestal of rock, battered by the buffetings of forty centuries, it stands, upspringing like a tongue of fire kindled of God to light the course of time down to its final goal and consummation.

OLD Time, himself so old, is like a child,
And can't remember when these blocks were piled
Or caverns scooped; but, with amazed eye,
He seems to pause, like other standers-by,
Half thinking how the wonders here made known
Were born in ages older than his own.

MODERN DISCOVERIES AND BIBLICAL CONNECTIONS.

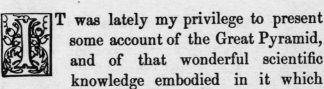

IT was lately my privilege to present some account of the Great Pyramid, and of that wonderful scientific knowledge embodied in it which has induced the belief that a higher wisdom than man's was concerned in its erection. I now resume the subject to present still other facts tending to the same conclusion.

A learned and able historical critic and lecturer recently stated to his audience in this city that what is thus claimed for the Great Pyramid may be true, and likely is true. And if such is the probability or even the possibility, the matter is not only worthy of our examination, but it would seem to be our duty to test it in every possible field of inquiry.

The theory is somewhat startling, and altogether so new and wonderful that some will doubtless be disposed to shrink from it as nothing but an extravagant fancy. It ought, however, to modify such a feeling when we remember that we live in an age of wonders, an age which answers well to the ancient prophecy of a time bordering on the end, when men would become great travellers and explorers, and as a consequence the stock of human knowledge be remarkably increased.

MODERN PROGRESS AND DISCOVERIES.

There certainly never was another period of such intense running to and fro in the earth or of such astounding growth in the range of human information as this in which we live. Events, inventions, and discoveries the most momentous crowd upon each other beyond our power to keep pace with them. Their multiplicity bewilders and confounds us. The whole life, condition, and dwelling-place of civilized man is being revolutionized by them. We travel now in palaces with every ease and luxury, and faster than the winds. We converse by electricity across oceans and continents. We spin, and knit, and weave, and print, and even calculate by automatic machinery. We copy nature and record her aspects by sunbeams. The whole world has become one neighborhood. Men have made visits to the poles, mapped the currents of the sea, belted the earth in every direction with lines of railroads and steamers, thrown down

the walls which for ages separated between
nations, brought all types and kindreds of men
face to face, and rendered a journey around the
globe a mere summer's recreation.

And especially in recoveries from the long-
forgotten past, in the reconstruction of history
before the historic periods, and in the bringing
to light of the wisdom and science of primeval ages, our times have been extraordinarily
rich and fruitful.   The last quarter of a century has been a very resurrection time in this
regard.   Ages of which we had only the dim-
mest hints have been marvellously recalled from
their oblivion.   With the ability to decipher
hieroglyphics and cuneiform inscriptions, old
worlds have newly opened to our contemplation.   By the mastery of languages, the tracing
of them to their primal sources and connections, the searching out and bringing together
of the scattered fragments of antiquity, and
the exhumation of ancient remains, the original migrations of the race have become traceable, and much of their long-lost history has
been reclaimed.   Things hitherto referred to
the department of myth, fable, and dream,
have suddenly assumed the character of authentic traditions. A little while ago, " Erech,
and Accad, and Calneh, in the land of Shinar,"

and Calah, and Resin of Asshur, and Ellasar,
and "Ur of the Chaldees," were mere names
in Genesis, with scarce another known trace
of them; but the mounds of Mesopotamia
have yielded up their bricks and stones to
modern research, and their long-silent tongues
have been loosed to tell where these places
stood and what mighty peoples once inhabited
them.   Babylon and Nineveh have thus un-
bosomed their records to testify how truly the
Bible spoke of them and what wealth, luxury, arrogance, and power once were theirs.
The names and exploits of their kings, their
conquests, their religions, their gods, their sciences, and their styles of life now stand in
many instances revealed before our eyes.
Arabia, till lately thought to be a mere desert
waste, and so marked on the maps, has disclosed grand seats of empire, with civilizations
once existent there superior even to Greece
and Rome.   Moab's rocks have become vocal
with attestations of the sacred records.   Ba-
shan's giant cities, and houses covered with
stone, and gates and doors of hinged rocks,
and walls and bars proportioned to their once
giant occupants, have been visited and their
ancient wonders verified.   Palestine has been
resurveyed, its old localities identified, and the

miracles of its history marvellously authenticated. Schliemann is uncovering Homeric cities and bringing up Homeric heroes and the old Homeric civilization out of their long-lost tombs. Even the whole way back through prehistoric ages to Nimrod and Noah is being laid open and lighted up by modern explorations. And why should it amaze us that from the land of Egypt also,—that land of oldest and most numerous monuments,—that land where nothing perishes,—that land so specially chosen of God as the theatre of his most stupendous miracles,—there should also be a bursting forth of unsuspected light to mingle some superior beams with the general illumination?

EGYPT'S PAST.

And if perchance these new disclosures should be of a character more sacred and imposing than what is being exhumed in other lands, it is what we might reasonably anticipate from a country so singularly linked with some of the most marvellous Divine administrations. It is a type of the world, indeed, but in its milder aspect; the darker type is Babylon. Even Bunsen tells us that Egypt has ever been the instrument for furthering the great designs of Providence. It has been at least the principal background of the most illustrious displays which have marked the career of God's chosen people. Israel could not become a nation without Egypt. The first and greatest of Israel's prophets was rescued from a watery grave, nurtured, schooled, and outwardly fitted for his sublime legation by the daughter of Egypt's king. Abraham himself, though from quite another section of the world, was ministered unto by Egypt. Joseph became the illustrious type of Christ by connection with Egypt. Humanly speaking, Jacob and his house would have come to a sad end had it not been for Egypt, which furnished him with bread, welcomed him to its richest lands, and gave his body a royal burial when he died. To Egypt's sovereign God sent that double dream of the kine and the ears of corn, which proved the means of Joseph's exaltation and of the salvation of so many peoples. Even when the blessed Jesus was born into our world Egypt was his asylum from the bloody sword of Herod, and once more and most literally of all were those words of Jehovah fulfilled, "Out of Egypt have I called my son." It was Egypt that gave to mankind the first translation of the

Hebrew Scriptures. It was Egypt that proved
the stronghold of Christianity after Jerusalem
fell. It is from Egypt that we have the
noblest and greatest fathers of the Christian
Church. And however ignoble now may be
the land or its population, we may rest assured
that God has something further to accomplish
by means of a country of which he has thus
availed himself in the past, and that out of it
will yet come some of the greatest of sacred
marvels which are to mark the closing periods
of time.

The Great Pyramid's Disclosures.

Some may doubt with regard to such antici-
pations; but they are already being realized
in the recent revelations of the Great Pyramid.
For forty centuries enshrouded in the deepest
mystery, that mighty pillar has at length begun
to yield up its secrets. As a mere building it
stands at the head of the world, in age, in
vastness of dimensions, in perfection of workmanship, and in the practical mastery of problems too hard for all our boasted modern art
and machinery. There is not an instance in
all the vast structure in which its architects
miscalculated or failed. They built for per-
manence. They planned their work to sur-

vive all the commotions of nature and all the
Vandalism of man.   Signally, also, have they
succeeded.   Not a stone necessary to its ulter-
ior purpose has come short of its office.   A
monument has thus come down to us from
beyond the classic ages which exalts and dig-
nifies the land in which it stands.   It is an
edifice of stones so wisely chosen, so justly
prepared, so wonderfully handled, so admirably joined, and in the proper places so
exquisitely cut and polished, that it is without
an equal in any land.   It is likewise pervaded
with the highest intelligence.   There is not
an inch of it which does not speak.   Even
after the lapse of four thousand years of observation, study, and experience, there is not
a nation or people whose wisdom or every-day
affairs it is not capable of improving.   There
is reason to think that we have not yet reached
the fulness of its grand symbolizations; but
if nothing more should come of the further
study of it, enough has been ascertained to
render it the most interesting problem of our
times.

The Pyramid and the Prophets.

It would also seem as if God's inspired
prophets knew of this marvellous pillar and

regarded it as a sacred wonder. The Greeks
as early as Alexander's time placed it at the
head of their list of "the seven wonders of
the world."   But Jeremiah before them wrote
of " signs and wonders in the land of Egypt,"
and of the placing of them there by "the
Great, the Mighty God, the Lord of hosts"
(Jer. 32 : 18–20), which would seem to refer to
this pyramid.   He was in Egypt when he
made this record.   He went there at the fall
of Jerusalem that he might write his prophecies and send them to his captive countrymen
in Babylon.   His method was to fortify his
testimony by appealing to all the records and
monuments which Jehovah had made of his
power and greatness in the earth.   He accordingly refers to " signs and wonders in the
land of Egypt," of which he says that they
still existed when he wrote,—"unto this day."
He is commonly thought to allude to the miracles of the Exodus, which certainly were
" signs and wonders " exactly to his purpose.
But those are specifically noted in a subsequent verse, and in phraseology better suited
to them.   The language here suggests something monumental, something locally fixed.
It naturally implies a Divine memorial, con-
tinuously abiding, and then still to be seen in

Egypt. It was something "set' there. The
word is the same in Hebrew and in English,
and with much the same sense in both.*   It
may be metaphorically used with regard to
miracles, but when used of things continuous
for hundreds of years after the placing, the
sense is cramped and strained when applied to
miracles like those of the Exodus, which disappeared with the relenting of Pharaoh and
the departure of Israel. So keenly has this
been felt that critics have been forced to speak
of a probable substitution of one word in place
of another, and men have cast about for some
remaining physical marks of the Mosaic miracles in order to satisfy the terms of the record.
Hence we read in Trapp's Commentary on the
passage, "Orosis writeth that the tracks of
Pharaoh's chariot-wheels are yet to be seen at
the Red Sea!" The Great Pyramid on the
new hypothesis would nobly help such critics
and commentators out of the mud, and grandly
meet the exact phraseology of the prophet.
Interpreted then by the most cogent laws of
language we here have a Scriptural recognition

---

* It is again and again rendered, *to make, to put, to cause to
be, to order, to appoint, to ordain, to place, to set up, to erect.*
Gesenius gives as its first and main sense, "*to set, to place, to
put, referring to persons or things which stand erect.*" Vatablus
translates it by *posuisti, placed, set up, erected, built.*

of some enduring monument in Egypt, built by God's appointment, and meant to be a witness to him.

Isaiah makes a similar reference of a still more circumstantial and positive character. In chap. 19 : 19, 20, he prophesies, " In that day shall there be an altar to the Lord in the midst of the land of Egypt, and a pillar at the border thereof to the Lord, and it shall be for a sign and for a witness unto the Lord of hosts in the land of Egypt."

This " altar" and "pillar" are not two things, but one and the same as sundry expositors have observed. The language is poetical, and has the common parallelism of Hebrew poetry. Given in the form and sense of the original, it would read

" In that day there is an altar to Jehovah
    In the midst of the land of Egypt;
Even a pillar at the border thereof to Jehovah,
And it shall be for a sign and witness to Jehovah of hosts
    In the land of Egypt."

Everything in this prophecy seems to look to the Great Pyramid. It refers to some specific and telling monument, and all its terms most fully apply to this marvellous pillar. There is nothing else known to which they do apply in literal accuracy and fulness.

Note how admirably the *titles* fit. "Altar"
in Hebrew means "the lion of God." The
Great Pyramid is pre-eminently the lion among
all earthly buildings, and the new theory
claims that it is Divine. The altar as described
by Ezekiel is largely pyramidal in form, and
is called "the mountain of God." And a
mountain, surely, is the Great Pyramid, and
one of a very remarkable character. The
sacred books of the Hindoos call it a mountain—*Rucm-adri*—"the golden mountain." It
is "a pillar," and hence not a sacrificial but
a memorial altar. It is a mammoth obelisk,—
one great individual shaft,—and now also
believed to be sacred.

The *location* likewise corresponds. The
Great Pyramid is the hub or centre of Egypt's
curved shoreline, and so is "in the midst of
the land," as nothing else to be thought of
ever was. Yet it is also "at the border thereof." It stands on the extreme southern limit
of Lower Egypt, and on the natural dividing
line between the two Egypts. It is thus
doubly "in the midst" and doubly "at the
border."

The *time* also answers. Six times the note
is sounded, and in every instance in the usual
Messianic and eschatological formula—"in

that day,"—a day which nowhere finally locates this side of the period of "the restitution
of all things." Whatever else the prediction
may cover, it cannot therefore be considered
exhausted yet, and necessarily brings us down
to the times bordering on the end. By per-
mission of Ptolemy Philometor, certain Jews
built a quasi temple and altar at Heliopolis,
which some take as the subject of the prophecy. But that erection was against the law
and could not be called Divine, though by
man's self-will intended to be so. Besides, that
was an altar of sacrifice and not a memorial
pillar as here described. Others think the
reference is to the establishment of churches
in Egypt, which were numerous in the early
Christian ages. But these properly had no
visible local altar at all, neither had they any
one monumental "pillar" to answer this description. When this altar gives forth its witness to Jehovah, Egypt, Assyria, and Israel
are to become a holy triad of divinely approved peoples, which has never yet occurred.
"A Saviour, and a great one," is then to come
to Egypt, and deliver from all oppressors. But
this is the language designating the glorious
Redeemer of the world, and we degrade and
profane it by applying it as some have done to

the pagan conqueror, Alexander. Christ, indeed, came to Egypt in his infancy, and afterwards in his Gospel, but never in the character of a national deliverer. We therefore look in vain for any true and exhaustive fulfilment of this prophecy in the past. It must refer to the latter times, and it fits to nothing known but the Great Pyramid. Even Vitringa, as early as the beginning of the last century, threw out the idea in his commentary on this place that some one or other of the existing monuments of Egypt is here involved.

THE PYRAMID AND THE BOOK OF JOB.

There is a still more distinct reference to the Great Pyramid in the Book of Job, 38 : 1–7. We there have one of the grandest descriptions in the Bible. The speaker is God, and the subject is the creation of the earth. The picture is the building of an edifice. Elsewhere in the book the earth is said to be hung upon nothing; so that we must not suppose ignorance of the real facts when the earth is here likened to a building resting on foundations. To overwhelm the pride of the human understanding, the Lord answered Job out of the whirlwind and said, "Who is this that darkeneth counsel by words without knowledge? Gird up now thy loins like a man, for I will demand of thee, and answer thou me. Where wast thou when I laid the foundations of the earth? Declare, if thou hast understanding. Who laid the measures thereof, if thou knowest? Or who hath stretched the line upon it? Whereupon are the foundations fastened [or "made to sink" as a seal into wax]? Or who laid the corner-stone thereof, when the morning stars sang together, and all the sons of God shouted for joy?"

"Behold here the architecture of God! The terms are those of the geometer—the master builder. Here are the bases, the joint-ings, the lines, the height, the corner-stone, the measures!" And the style of the building is unquestionably the Pyramid. That "corner-stone" spoken of in the singular, its emphatic isolation from "the foundations," and the singing and shouting of the heavenly hosts over the mighty achievement at the laying of that particular stone, require the proper py-ramidal edifice. The picture will not interpret of anything else. That corner-stone could not be at the base,* for others were there against

---

* This is also distinctly expressed in the ancient Coptic ver-sion, translated by Archdeacon Tattam. There in the sixth verse the language is, "Who hath laid the corner stone *upon*

which no such marked distinction in truth
existed, and its laying would then have been
at the beginning, at which time this celestial
celebration would be out of place. Even
Barnes, contrary to the erroneous imagery by
which he tries to interpret the passage, agrees
that " the time referred to is *at the close* of the
creation of the earth." And as this celebration according to God himself is at the laying
of that corner-stone, it must needs be a top
stone—a corner-stone at the summit—whose
laying completed the edifice and showed the
whole work in finished perfection. But for
such a corner-stone at the summit there is no
place in any then known form of building,
save only the Pyramid, of which it is characteristic.

Nor is it only to the pyramidal form in
general that the allusion is, but to a particular
pyramid. By that strange reference to the
sunken feet or planting of the foundations in
" sockets," we are conducted directly to the
Great Pyramid of Gizeh. Two socketed " encastrements," " socles," shoes, or incised sinkings

---

it ?" If a base corner-stone were in contemplation it would be
in place to speak of the placing of the building upon it ; but
only a top or summit corner-stone can be said to be laid
" upon " the building, and no building has such a top corner-
stone but the Pyramid.

into the rock were found under two of its base corners by the French *savants* in 1799, which were again uncovered and described by Colonel Howard Vyse, in 1837. And as God here speaks of such a fastening down of the foundations in general, Prof. Smyth was persuaded that there were corresponding "sockets" at the other two base corners, and when search was made for them in 1865, they were found by Messrs. Aiton and Inglis, assisted by Prof. Smyth. Here then are the whole four "sockets" or fastened foundations. Nothing of the sort exists at any other known pyramid. They are among the distinctive marks of the Great Pyramid of Gizeh. They are the enduring tracks of its feet cut into the living rock, by which Almighty God himself identifies it for us as the original image from which his own description of the creation is drawn. Men may treat the matter as they will, but here are the facts showing a Divine recognition of this particular edifice as the special symbol of the earth's formation !

And from the same passage we also get some important rays of Divine light with regard to the builders of this pillar and their estimate of it.

The singers and shouters at the completion

of the earth's creation of course were heavenly
intelligences, as most expositors agree in teaching.   But as the laying of the capstone of the
Great Pyramid is divinely given as the symbol of the laying of the capstone in the fabric
of our world, the singers and their rejoicings
so sublimely referred to in the one case must
also have had place in the other.

It is never to be overlooked that there are
earthly " morning stars " and " sons of God "
as well as heavenly ones.   " As many as are
led by the Spirit of God, they are the sons of
God."   There were such " sons of God " on
earth before the flood.   Adam was one of them,
and his immediate descendants in the line of
Seth were others.   Many of them apostatized,
but some remained faithful.   Noah was one of
those faithful ones, and he was brought over
the great water bearing with him all the sacred
rites, traditions, and revelations of his holy
fathers.   By him the newly baptized world
began once more.   From his coming out of
the ark to the building of the Great Pyramid,
the call of Abraham, and the commission of
Moses, was really the morning time of our present world.   Like other mornings it had its
noble " stars " and " sons of God " who shone
with patriarchal faithfulness and glorious tes-

timony in their time.   Shem and numbers of
his seed at least were of this class.   Job, and
Melchisedec, and Abraham were pre-eminent
among them.   Jehovah has always had a people of his own among men, a people who reflected his mind and will, preserved his revelations, obeyed his commands, and kept to the
pure worship of his name.   Even long after
the call of Abraham there was yet a true
" priest of the Most High God " in Palestine,
and another in Midian, and inspired Gentile
prophets as late as the days of Moses and
Aaron.   These were God's " sons " by faith in
him and " stars " of light amid the darkness
of those early times—noble harbingers of the
coming day.

Such " morning stars " and " sons of God "
were on the earth when the Great Pyramid
was built, corresponding to those in heaven
when the earth was made.   And as the one
structure is the symbol of the other, even to
its most hidden mysteries and measures, the
analogy would be singularly incomplete in one
of the most significant features of the divinely
drawn parallel if the singing and shouting did
not occur in one case as in the other.

But if these early light-bearers and children
of God on earth sung and shouted at the lay-

ing of the capstone of the Great Pyramid as
the heavenly hosts sung and shouted when the
fabric of the world was completed, they must
needs have understood it and been in deepest
sympathy with it. It must have been identified with their most sacred thoughts and con-
templations. It must have been of a character
in full and glorious accord with what distinguished them from other people and made them
" stars " and " sons of God." It must have
been something most profoundly related to
Jehovah and the holy treasures of his ancient
revelations and promises, and hence not a mere
obtrusive tomb got up by some proud, oppressive, and beast-worshipping worldly tyrant.

From the Book of God itself we thus legitimately gather that the Great Pyramid did not
originate with idolatrous Egypt; that it connects with the most precious things of those
" sons of God" who shone as lights in the dim
morning of the world's history; that it was
the subject of their devoutest joy and grati-
tude; and that in their esteem it was everything which it is now supposed to be.

THE PYRAMID AND CHRIST.

But then we would expect it also to refer to
Christ and redemption. The great subject of

all sacred Revelation is the Christ and his glorious kingdom, and we can hardly suppose this pillar Divine if it has not something on this point. Men may well sneer at the idea of a special revelation to old Cheops or his architects to teach the diameter, density, and temperature of the earth. Something of mightier moment to mankind must be involved when Jehovah thus interposes. Such claims need to be tried by the pre-eminent theme of all inspiration. But even on this high ground the Great Pyramid sustains itself full as grandly as in the sphere of cosmic facts and geodetic measures.

When Zerubbabel and Jeshua were engaged rebuilding Jerusalem and the Temple on the return from the great captivity, they had in hand a work of extraordinary greatness, difficulty, and discouragements. So important was it in itself, and so bound up in history and type with another and greater restoration, that it was made the occasion and subject of special Divine communication through Zechariah the prophet. And in those prophecies that work and all that it typified is set forth under the image of the building of the Pyramid. A "great mountain" of worldly power and difficulty was in the way, but God said it should

become "a plain before Zerubbabel," as the
Gizeh hill was levelled to receive the Great
Pyramid. As despite all hindrances the Pyramid was successfully carried forward to completion, even to the laying of the peculiar
corner-stone of its apex amid the songs of
"the morning stars" and the shouts of "all
the sons of God," so was Zerubbabel and he
whom Zerubbabel typified to succeed in their
Divine work, even to the "bringing forth of
the headstone thereof with shoutings, crying,
'Grace, Grace unto it.'" (Zech. 4 : 6, 7.) The
pyramid idea is absolutely essential to an intelligible and consistent interpretation of this
imagery. The picture is an exact parallel to
the one in Job, only transferred from nature
to grace,—from geologic to Messianic territory.

By necessary implications of Holy Scripture
then the Great Pyramid is immutably linked
with the building of the Church of which the
adorable Jesus is "the headstone," "the chief
corner-stone."

It is also a clear and outstanding fact that
the Scriptures continually make the pyramid
capstone the type and symbol of Christ, both
in the Old Testament and in the New. Who
needs to be reminded with what brilliant dic-
tion Moses likens Jehovah to a rock, and how

triumphantly he asserts against all the heathen world, that " their rock is not as our rock, even our enemies themselves being judges !" Out of the very spirit as well as letter of the Holy Book every Christian congregation using the English tongue, often lifts up its voice to Jesus, singing

> Rock of ages, cleft for me,
> Let me hide myself in thee!

He is not only such a rock as that which yielded thirsty Israel drink, or as that which gives the weary traveller shelter from the scorching sunshine or beating storm, or as that which the prudent builder seeks whereon to found his house securely, but especially such a rock as that which forms the apex of the Pyramid—a rock which is the head and crown of all the works of Providence and grace—the unique bond in which the whole edifice of time is united—the headstone of redemption lifted high above all other rocks, " that in all things he might have the pre-eminence." So David conceived of him when he sung, " The stone which the builders refused is become the headstone of the corner," or " the head corner-stone," as the Septuagint renders it. (Ps. 118 : 22.) So Peter being

"filled with the Holy Ghost," conceived of
him when he said to the Jews who had con-
demned and crucified him, " This is the stone
which was set at naught by you builders
which is become the head of the corner."
(Acts 4 : 11.)   Hence, also, he wrote to his
scattered brethren in the faith as having come
to Jesus, "as unto a living stone disallowed
indeed of men, but chosen of God, and precious," in whom they also " as lively stones
were built up a spiritual house," according to
the saying of God, " Behold I lay in Zion a
chief corner-stone, elect, precious," even "the
stone which the builders disallowed," but
which now "is made the head of the corner,
and a stone of stumbling and a rock of
offence even to them which stumble at the
word." (1 Pet. 2 : 4–8.)   So Paul conceived
of him when he wrote to the Ephesians, ". Ye
are built upon the foundation of the apostles
and prophets, Jesus Christ himself being the
chief corner-stone, in whom all the building
fitly framed together groweth unto an holy
temple in the Lord, in whom ye also are
builded together for an habitation of God
through the spirit." (Eph. 2 : 20–22.)   And
the same conception Jesus applied to himself
when he said, " Did ye never read in the

Scriptures, the stone which the builders rejected the same is become the head of the
corner? And whosoever shall fall on this
stone shall be broken, but on whomsoever it
shall fall it will grind him to powder." (Matt.
21 : 42–44.)

All these are great central passages of the
Divine word, and not one of them will interpret without the Pyramid, whose light alone
brings out their full significance and beauty.
It is absurd enough when men speak of a
river's head at one end of it, and its mouth at
the other end ; but it is unbearable to represent the Holy Ghost treating of the head of a
thing as in its toes. Interpreters may put
such absurdities in the Bible, but its author
never does. The head is not the foot nor the
foot the head in any consistent or intelligible
use of language. So the head corner-stone
cannot be the foot or foundation corner-stone.
Where there are four alike, to regard one as
chief is a mere conventionalism without reality in fact, and such as the Bible never em-
ploys. Common architecture furnishes no one
pre-eminent corner or corner-stone. There is
no head corner without the Pyramid. That
alone has such a head at the head, or a corner-
stone uniquely and indisputably the chief. It

has the usual four at the base, alike in shape, place and office, but it has a fifth, different from all others and far more exalted. It is at the top, and properly the head one. It is the last to come into place and so may be long rejected while the building still goes on. The base corner-stones must be laid at the beginning. Work cannot proceed while either of them is disallowed. They are also of such regular shape as renders them capable of being worked in as well at one place as at another. They furnish no occasion to be disallowed. Not so the head corner-stone. The shape of that is altogether peculiar. It is five-sided and five-pointed. From foundation to summit there is no place at which it will fit till everything else is finished and its own proper place is reached. Till then it is naturally enough rejected by the builders. They have no place for it. To those ignorant of its purpose it is only in the way—"a rock of offence and a stone of stumbling." With one sharp point always sticking upwards, any one falling on it would necessarily "be broken." And when on its way to its position hundreds of feet in the air were it to fall on any one it would certainly "grind him to powder."

But though rejected to the last, it finally

turns out to be the very thing required, and
reaches a place to which it alone fits; a place
above all others, where it sublimely finishes
out and binds together everything in one
glorious whole. It is itself a perfect pyramid,
the original model of the edifice which it com-
pletes and adorns. It is emphatically the head
stone of the head corner. It is at the head
and not at the feet. It has its own peculiar
angles and they are the angles of the entire
structure. There is but one stone of that
shape and it is the shape of the pyramid complete. It is the stone which stands toward
Heaven for every other in the building. Every
other stone in all the mighty construction
stands in it, and has place with reference to it,
and is touched by its weight and influence, as
well as sheltered under its lines, and honored
and perfected by its presence. It is indeed
the " all in all " of the whole edifice. To its
angles is " all the building fitly framed together." And in it every part and particle that
belongs to the structure from foundation to
capstone has its bond of perfectness, its shelter,
and its crown.

About such imagery there should be no
question. In all the richness of the Scriptures there is not a more luminous, expressive,

and comprehensive picture of the Christ, in himself, in his experiences, in his relations to his friends or foes, in his office and place in all the dispensations of God toward our race, than that which is given in these texts when studied in the light of the Great Pyramid. These passages alone consecrate and sanctify it forever. In them the Holy Ghost takes hold of it, traces in it a sacred significance, and assigns to it relations and connections, the truth and beauty of which cannot be disputed. And thus by the highest authority known to man it is rendered impossible to be thoroughly true to the utterances of inspiration, and yet regard this venerable monument as nothing but the profane tomb of a pagan despot.

The Pyramid and the Christian Dispensation.

And this sublime testimony to the Great Pyramid from without is also fully sustained by its own testimony from within. We have seen in a former lecture how grandly it symbolizes the truths of nature. Let us glance now at its symbolizations of Grace.

Prof. Smyth relates that in the course of the summer of 1872, Mr. Charles Casey, of Pollerton Castle, Carlow, wrote him that while he had followed and adopted all the explanations as to the metrology of the Great Pyramid being of more than human scientific perfection for the age in which it was produced,—yet to call it therefore divinely inspired or " sacred " seemed to him to be either too much or too little. " Now, said Mr. Casey, unless the Great Pyramid can be shown to be Messianic as well as fraught with superhuman science and design, its ' sacred ' claim is a thing with no blood in it,—nothing but mere sounding brass." Nor was this an unreasonable test. And it is one which I am happy to say the Great Pyramid very nobly stands.

The first to break ground in this department was Robert Menzies, a young shipbuilder and draughtsman, of Leith, Scotland, a Christian Israelite who never saw the Great Pyramid, but had long been engaged in the devout study of the works which describe it. In 1865 he wrote to Prof. Smyth that the immense superiority of the height and finish of the Grand Gallery over every other passage is owing to the fact that it represents the Christian dispensation, while the other passages symbolize only human histories or preparatory dispensations. He also had good reason for this conclusion, more perhaps than he knew.

The Christian dispensation by common con-

sent dates from the birth of Christ. If the
Grand Gallery represents it, then the mark for
the birth of Christ is the commencement of
that gallery. The unit or that which counts
one in pyramid measure is the inch, and so the
inch, as in the diagonals of the base, symbolizes the grand unit of time, a year, at least in
the floorlines of the passages taken as scrolls
of history. Measuring thirty-three inches
then from the beginning of the Grand Gallery
for the duration of the earthly life of Christ,
we come precisely over against the mouth of
that mysterious " well " with its ramp-stone
cover gone, as if violently forced out from
beneath. That "well" extends irregularly
down through the masonry and rock to a wide
cavern, and thence to the entrance of the
bottomless pit itself. It is a striking symbol
of death, sealing up in the sepulchre, descent
into hell, and triumphant resurrection in irresistible power. And it comes at a place to
fit precisely to the death and resurrection of
our blessed Lord. This certainly is a very
strong point with which to begin.

The Christian dispensation is emphatically
the dispensation of new life. Its pervading
spirit is that of resurrection. Basing itself on
the resurrection of Christ as its great sealing

fact, it went everywhere in the power of the Holy Ghost awakening men out of their moral graves and calling them forth in a new birth, " that like as Christ was raised from the dead by the glory of the Father, even so we also should walk in newness of life." Most intensely also is this signified throughout the whole length of the Grand Gallery of our Pyramid. It is lined along its base on both sides with ramp-stones like " washboards" to a stairway. They are about a foot high and wide, and they are all cut with miniature symbolic graves every one of which is open. More than this, right by the side of each of these open graves is a neatly cut stone set vertically in the wall. It is a symbol of standing upright, and almost audibly proclaims the tenants of those open graves risen, as all true Christians are, not only from the death of sin, but to an heirship of a still completer resurrection through him who is to come again. There are eight times seven of these open graves. Eight is the number of new life and resurrection, and seven of dispensational fulness, so that by their numbers they also signify this newness of life. We thus have one of the intensest and most spiritual features of the Gospel as emphatically pronounced as stones can speak it.

The Christian dispensation is likewise pictured in the Bible as made up of seven churches headed by "seven stars" which are "the angels of the seven churches." So the best and earliest commentators explain that first vision of the Apocalypse, which allows very little room for differences of opinion. And a corresponding symbol of the same is contained in this Grand Gallery. It stares every one in the face the moment the place is entered. All writers have described it as one of the peculiar beauties of the singular arrangement. Each side of the wall is made up of just seven courses of finely fitted polished stones, the one overlapping the other and extending the whole length from commencement to termination. It is the gallery of the seven courses just seven times the height of the other passages. Besides, this gallery has special relations to the Pleiades. It tells in several ways of those benignant and exalted stars. In its own way it thus also points to the "seven stars" as presiding over the seven churches.

As a matter of historic fact the Christian dispensation followed immediately on the Jewish economy, of which it is the crown and completion. The law leads the way to Christ. This historical succession is also carefully pre-

served in the symbolizations of our Pyramid.
The first upward passage which leads to the
Grand Gallery is just the number of inches in
length which the best chronologists give as the
number of years from the Exodus to the birth
of Christ.   It is the way to the Grand Gallery
as the Jewish dispensation is the way to the
Christian.

The Christian dispensation also has a fixed
limit.   It is to terminate with the coming
again of the Lord Jesus to judge the quick
and the dead.   Every commission under which
we now act extends only to that time.   And
that coming of Christ to end this age is everywhere presented as impending,—as a thing
which might occur any day.   All this is likewise symbolized in the Grand Gallery of the
Great Pyramid. Its termination is as distinctly
marked as its beginning, and even the impend-
ingness of the end is not overlooked.   Its
south or further wall leans a full degree and
overhangs its base as if it might fall at any
moment.

From my studies of the Apocalypse, I was
led to publish years ago my firm belief that
the present Church period is to be succeeded
by a dispensation of judgment extending
through years before the great consummation

is reached. And here we have it most evidently symbolized next after the end of the Grand Gallery. There the passage becomes low again, for the Church as such has ended its career. There the "granite leaf"—a great frowning double stone—hangs in its grooves, beneath which every one that passes in must bow, exhibiting a most impressive picture of "the great tribulation" of the judgment period. There also are the rules and measures by which the Pyramid was constructed, all graven on the stones, indicative of the complete righting up of everything according to law and justice. And then only comes the entrance into the grand and polished granite chamber of the king.

One of the most exalted steps in the history of the Church is that which was accomplished during the first quarter of our present century. It was in the first twenty-five years since 1800 that Christendom throughout the world formed its great organizations for the dissemination of the Holy Scriptures, for the publication and general diffusion of religious literature and Gospel truth, and for the sending out and support of missionaries to the heathen, to plant the Church of Jesus in all lands and islands. It was in those years that the Christian world

experienced a revival of aggressive evangelization and missionary zeal, the greatest and
the most general since the days of the Apostles,
the effects of which continue with still increasing power.   The coming into activity of these
organizations with their results was so marked
an advance on everything of the kind for more
than twelve hundred years, and so universal
that we might justly expect it to be noted in
any complete prophetic symbolization of our
dispensation.   Accordingly following the floor-
line of the Pyramid's Grand Gallery towards
its upper end we come to a grand step three
feet high.   I long wondered what it could
mean, as it is the only one in the whole length
of the glorious passage after that somewhat
corresponding rise not far from the beginning.
But when I came to count the number of
inches from the commencement of the Grand
Gallery to this upper step the mystery was
solved.   The number of those inches is close
about one thousand eight hundred and fourteen,
which at the rate of an inch for a year brings
us to the very centre of those years in which
the Church universal made this mighty, and
unexampled stride.   Beyond this step there
is no further ascent.   The great stone which
forms it is also the weakest and most frac-

tured and dilapidated of all the stones in the whole passage-way of the Grand Gallery. It shows a marvellous rise, but an equally marvellous absence of solidity and strength. It is the image of brokenness, feebleness, and the want of firm texture. It seems as if crumbling away under the feet of those who stand upon it. And this again most strikingly accords with the poor, rent, weak, and wasting character of the Christianity of our times, though they be times of universal evangelization. It is Christianity, and evinces a great rise in effort and aim ; but it is a very shattered and infirm Christianity, with but little solid substance left and incapable of enduring long.

Thus there is scarce a feature of our dispensation from the birth of Christ till now, or that is anywhere foretold of its end, which is not symbolized in the Grand Gallery of the Great Pyramid. Man in all his ingenuity is incompetent to devise a simpler and completer chart of it, were he to labor at it for ages. And yet here it is in all its great facts, characteristics, and relations, in its beginning and end, in its constitution and history, in what went before and in what comes after, built into an edifice of mighty rocks more than three times

seven hundred years before Christ was born.
All this certainly is very remarkable.

Is it then within the reason of man to say
that there was nothing above and beyond mere
human power and calculation here,—no potent
presence of that MIND which knows the end
of all things from the beginning, and giveth
wisdom unto the wise?

THE PYRAMID AND THEOLOGY.

Tested also by the more inward substance
and contents of sound Scriptural doctrine, the
facts are equally remarkable and cogent.

The foundation of all sacred doctrines is
the existence of a personal and eternal God,
the Almighty Maker of heaven and earth.
The Bible pronounces that man a "fool"—one
criminally self-stultified—who can find it in
his heart to say, "there is no God." So also
the Great Pyramid teaches. It symbolizes the
earth and all the universe as a contrivance, a
work, a building, shaped to Promethean plan.
It must therefore have had a contriver, an intelligent and potent author, greater than itself.
It thus pronounces at one and the same time
against Atheism, against Sabaism, against
Pantheism, and against all idolatry and false
worship. It knows nothing of a world with-

out an architect, of creaturehood without basis
or centre, of beauty without parent or birth-
place, of good without a bosom out of which it
flows, of thought without reason, of effect without a cause.   It proclaims the universe a prod-
uct, and one self-competent God as its author.

It is an essential part of orthodox theology
that Jehovah is a three-one God.   " The true
Christian faith is this, that we worship one
God in Trinity, and Trinity in Unity, neither
confounding the persons nor dividing the substance."   And when we ascribe glory to the
Father, and to the Son, and to the Holy Ghost,
we rightfully add " as it was in the beginning,"
for so is the representation in this Pyramid
before the Bible was written.   On each of its
four faces as in its fundamental figure it presents to every beholder the geometric emblem
of the Trinity, the same that is accepted by
the Church and exhibited in nearly every
place of Christian worship.   Creation is the
reflection of God himself, and the Pyramid as
a symbol of the creation gives impressive token
of His mysterious Tri-unity.   Nature reflects
Trinity, and this symbol of nature does the
same with a depth and stress which cannot be
disputed.   Shaw states that the Deity is typified by the outward form of this pile, and that

form is a triangle whether viewed on either side or from either corner.

The architect of the world this monument likewise proclaims to be the *King* of the world, a governing and upholding Providence as well as a tri-personal Creator. Those measures, motions, interrelations, and vast revolutions which it symbolizes, all tell that the universe does not hold God but that thus he holds and manages the universe. They are the grasp and pressure of an infinite and Almighty hand, whose fingers clasp the crystal poles of the earth and heavens, and under whose protecting palm the continents and seas, planets, suns, and systems pass with unfaltering steadiness from age to age. And the conformation of its shape, measures, avenues, and openings, to cosmic and celestial facts, themselves the symbols of an eternal Providence, proclaims the potent presence of God in the histories as well as in the constitution of the earth.

But the Bible tells also of an evil power in the universe—an anti-God—whom it describes as an apostate angelic being who has obtained a terrible influence over the affairs and destiny of man. He is called the Dragon, the old Serpent, Satan, the Devil. He is declared to be a murderer, a tempter, a destroyer, a liar, the author of all evil, under whose usurped dominion mankind, unhelped of God, are hopelessly inthralled. And this too is strikingly expressed by the Great Pyramid.

From the earliest known times different portions of the heavens have been designated, and known by certain figures supposed to be outlined by the stars which they embrace. There are now about eighty of these constellations. The stars of which they are composed the Bible declares to be for "signs," as well as for seasons, days, and years. The probability is that the earlier and most remarkable of these designations were made by God himself even before the flood. Josephus attributes the invention of the constellations to the family of Seth, the son of Adam, and refers to ancient writers as authorities. Origen affirms that it was asserted in the Book of Enoch that in the time of that patriarch the constellations were already divided and named.* Vol-

---

* The Book of Enoch, translated by Bishop Lawrence, is as a whole, an apocryphal production, dating somewhere about the beginning of the reign of Herod, before Christ. It has some ten chapters devoted to the mysteries of astronomy, the heavenly bodies, and their relations and revolutions. It will at least serve to show what was the feeling on the part of those whom the writer represents when he says that all these things were made known to Enoch by Uriel, the holy angel, who gave "the whole account of them according to every year of the

ney informs us that everywhere in antiquity
there was a cherished tradition of an expected
conqueror of the serpent, and asserts that this
tradition is reflected in the constellations as
well as in all the heathen mythologies. Du-
puis, also, and others of his school have collected ancient authorities abundantly proving
that in all nations this tradition always pre-
vailed, and that the same is represented in the
constellations. Indeed, antiquity with one
voice declares for their very early origin, and
the results of modern investigations by astronomers themselves confirm the traditions and
reveal internal evidence of their having been
constructed more than five thousand years
ago. Cassini commences his *History of Astronomy* by saying, " It is impossible to doubt
that astronomy was invented from the beginning of the world; history profane as well as
sacred testifies to this truth." Bailly and
others assert that astronomy must have been
established when the summer solstice was in
the first degree of Virgo, and that the solar
and lunar zodiacs were of a similar antiquity,

---

world forever, until a new work (or creation) shall be effected
which will be eternal." The twelve signs of the Zodiac are
plainly indicated in this book. See Book of Enoch, chap. 71,
seq., pp. 84, 85, and 232.

which would be about four thousand years
before the Christian era. They suppose the
originators to have lived in about the fortieth
degree of north latitude, and to have been a
highly civilized people. Prof. Proctor, by calculations based on Hindoo and other astronomies, traces the authors of this science to
some people residing between the rivers Cyrus
and Araxas, not very far from Mount Ararat,
at a date perhaps two thousand two hundred
years before Christ. Sir William Drummond
says, " The fact is certain that at some remote
period there were mathematicians and astronomers who knew that the sun is the centre of
our system, and that the earth itself a planet
revolves around it." The constellations were
certainly known in the time of Job, and are
familiarly referred to in that very ancient
book. Seyffarth says they are as old as the
human race. The author of *Mazzaroth* makes
the origin of the constellations antediluvian,
and thinks they were framed by inspiration
for sacred and prophetic purposes. There are
actual astronomical calculations in existence
with calendars formed upon them, which eminent astronomers of England and France
admit to be genuine and true, and which carry
back the antiquity of this science together

with the constellations to within a few years of
the deluge, even on the longer chronology of
the Septuagint. Sir John Herschel finds much
fault with these old constellations as barbarous
and unscientific. He would have these con-
torted snakes, miscalled bears, lions, fishes,
and the like, banished from our astronomies
as too oppressive to the student's memory.
But the author of *Mazzaroth* very well suggests
that this learned astronomer perhaps never
came across the proper meaning of these gro-
tesque figures or never duly studied them as
symbols, or he would have been less anxious
for their obliteration. Nay, the specimens
which modern astronomers have given of their
skill at such reforms do not much recommend
the giving of free scope to them in this particular. The universality of these ancient
groupings must ever secure their retention,
however disliked by scientists. And the very
inconvenience of them for naked astronomical
purposes is proof not of the barbarism of their
inventors, but that they were meant to serve
some further end. The most important historical, theological, and prophetic truths have
been inscribed on the heavens by means of
them, so that they need only to be stripped of
the changes, caricatures, and interpolations of

the heathen Greeks and modern scientists in
order to show us the outlines of the Bible on
the sky, and to prove that in a high, evangelic,
and most impressive sense "the heavens declare the glory of God." The author of *Mazzaroth* and others have not only said but
shown that we have in these ancient constellations a medium of communication with the
mind, theology, and hopes of primitive man,
and that we here may read the fact that God
has spoken to our race, given to it a Revelation
from the beginning, and embodied in it precisely the same great truths afterwards written
and developed in the sacred Scriptures. Everywhere do we encounter the traditions of Abraham's skill in the knowledge of the heavens,
how he argued from his observations of the
heavenly orbs, and how he occupied himself
in Egypt teaching the priests of Heliopolis in
the lore of the skies. Doubtless this was not
the naked science of astronomy as the schools
conceive of it, but as respected the theological
and Messianic truths symbolized in these celestial hieroglyphics, in which, as in the more
literal promises, he rejoiced to see Christ's day,
and saw it and was glad. (John 8 : 56.)
Well, therefore, has it been that these ancient
"signs" have been preserved. And mankind

have reason to pray that no hand of intermeddling science may ever sweep them down, but that they may continue to stand unto the end in all the almanacs of time.

One of the oldest and most universal of these ancient constellations is the Dragon or Great Serpent. The chief star embraced in that group (a Draconis) is situated in the monster's tail. And to that star the entrance passage of the Great Pyramid was levelled, so that a Draconis at its lower culmination then looked right down that inclined tube to the bottomless pit. Mankind marching down that passage would therefore be moving under the sign and dominion of the Dragon. Thus in a manner which startles by its vividness the Great Pyramid answers to the Bible in saying that there is a Devil, who has somehow obtained an awful potency over the human race, and that mankind under him are on the way to the pit of destruction. The picture is that of a tube over which the Dragon presides, whose incline is fearfully downwards, and which terminates in hell! Could the story be told in simpler or more graphic terms?

Some laugh at the idea of a hell. Even whole denominations calling themselves Christians make it a point of faith to deny the existence of any such thing. But the Bible tells about it as a dark and mysterious underworld—a bottomless pit—a subterranean region of hopeless misery,—out of which there is no escape. And here is the symbol of it in the Great Pyramid—a room far under the centre of the edifice, one hundred feet down in the solid rock, having neither bottom nor outlet. It has continuity in a tube on the further side, but it is endless, the same as the pit is bottomless. With singular significance has this feature been copied in all other pyramids, to whose hopeless subterranean chambers the kings of idolatrous and self-justifying Egypt were consigned. Hence the words of Ezekiel (31 : 14–18): " They are all delivered unto death, to the nether parts of the earth, in the midst of the children of men, with them that go down to the pit. . .   This is Pharaoh and all his multitude, saith the Lord God." And in the facile and smooth descent of that main passage-way leading directly down to the pit we have the symbol of the tendency and hopeless destiny of man since his fall into Satan's power, except as recovered by some gracious intervention superior to nature and mightier than the Devil.

But the glad and glorious teaching of the

Bible is that God has interposed, introduced a new and saving economy, calling Abraham, commissioning and inspiring Moses and the prophets, establishing for himself a consecrated people, and preparing the way for a sublime Deliverer in Jesus Christ, who has brought forgiveness and eternal life into the world, and arranged for a new and eternal dominion of righteousness and peace, which is to dethrone Satan and bring man back to original blessedness. This is the very soul and spirit of the Scriptures—the master theme of both Testaments and of all their institutes. And the same is the great subject of all the chief parts of the Great Pyramid's interior—the burden of its noblest passages—the story of all its upper apartments.

The first ascending passage begins at the point which answers in the number of its year-inches to the date of the Exodus of Israel. It also covers by its length the precise number of inches that there were years from the Exodus to the birth of Christ. We thus identify it as the Pyramid's symbol of the Mosaic dispensation. That dispensation was an upward movement in human history founded on direct supernatural interferences of the Almighty, and so this is an upward passage with the same angle heavenward as that of the entrance passage is hellward. It is a most expressive symbol of a special and effective interposition of God to raise men up from their decline toward destruction, and thus furnishes us with a monumental testimony to the whole Scriptural representation of that economy.

But the Mosaic dispensation was only intermediate and preliminary to something greater and higher. Hence that upward passage suddenly enlarges into a far more magnificent ascending opening. The top abruptly rises to seven times the previous height, and everything is correspondingly exalted into the Grand Gallery. This is the symbol of the Christian era—the grandest section in all the scrolls of human history. It begins at the inch which marks the Saviour's birth. Thirty-three inches from that beginning bring us to the startling symbol of death, burial, descent into hell, and resurrection from the dead,—to that fearful "well" with its heavy stone covering broken out by an upward force which tore away a part of the wall itself, "for it was not possible that he should be holden of death." The entire length is covered with thirty-six overspanning stones, the number of months of Christ's public ministry. And beyond is

the granite King's Chamber in which all con-
summates.   And there the polished walls,
fine materials, grand proportions, and exalted
place, eloquently tell of glories yet to come.
It is the chamber of fifties, which is the grand
jubilee number.

Nay, for those Gentiles who never knew of
Israel's worship and sacred books there is also
a word of hope inserted.   They are not necessarily all lost.   From the lowest depths of
Ethnic apostasy the Great Pyramid still indicates a way up through the atoning death of
Christ to the celestial blessedness.   It is a
steep, tortuous, difficult, dangerous, and un-
certain way, not likely to be found and safely
traversed by many; but it is there.   It is a
speaking symbol of what the inspired Apostle
declared so long afterwards, that " in every
nation he that feareth God and worketh right
eousness is accepted of him," accepted through
the mediation of Christ.

Here are symbolizations of sacred histories
whose warp and woof is miracle.   Here are
expressions the soul of which is the same
Divine breath which animates and fills the
Testaments of God.   Here are heavenward
pointings and indications of the way to eternal
life as distinct and gracious as those which

mark the holy Evangely itself. It is the
Gospel pronounced in stone. It is the testimony of "Jesus and the resurrection" put up
in imperishable rock. It is redemption memorialized in marble more than twenty centuries before the Christ was born! Could it
be mere accident? Was it not rather the dear
God above us laying up the sublime things
of his grace in enduring lithic records which
man could not alter nor time destroy to demonstrate to the skeptics of our day how unreasonable and inexcusable is their unbelief?

The Pyramid and the Day of Judgment.

The Bible moreover tells of a nearing day
of judgment—a time when the Almighty
power that made us will reckon with us concerning these earthly lives of ours, and deal
out destiny according to the uses we have made
of them. In all its addresses, whether didac-
tic or prophetic,—whether to warn the wicked
or comfort the pious,—whether for the vindica-
tion of God or the foreshadowing of what is to
become of man,—the Bible everywhere refers
us to an approaching crisis, when the principles
of eternal justice must go into full effect, when
the trampled law will inexorably enforce its
supremacy, when everything must be righted

up, and all that is adverse to truth and good be forever blasted; when faith and virtue shall be rewarded and enthroned, and all else sink overwhelmed by a majesty which nothing can withstand. It is described as a time of sorrow and unexampled distress for the unbelieving world—a time of fears and plagues and great tribulation to all but God's watching and ready ones, to whom it shall be a day of glorious coronation in heaven. Its coming is spoken of as sudden—when men in general do not expect it—when many are saying, " Peace and safety." Like the flood upon the old world—like the tempest of hail and fire which overwhelmed Sodom and Gomorrah—so shall it come upon the nations. When men think not, the Son of man cometh. And all this too is solemnly pronounced by the Great Pyramid. That Grand Gallery stops abruptly. It is suddenly cut off in its continuity. From a splendid passage-way twenty-eight feet in height it ceases instantly, and the further passage is less than four feet. The floorline then no longer ascends. A ponderous double block of frowning granite, hard and invincible, hangs loose over the low and narrow pass now. In the same antechamber in which it hangs, the rules, measures, and weights appear engraven

in majesty upon the imperishable granite, for
every one to pass under.   The tokens are that
now judgment is laid to the line, and righteousness to the plummet, that every cover may
be lifted, and every refuge of lies swept away.
Everything here indicates the inexorable ad-
judications of eternal righteousness.

And that solemn time is also everywhere
represented as now close at hand.   As far as
theologians have been able to ascertain, all the
prophetic dates are about run out.   The Scriptural signs of the end have appeared.   Every
method of computation points to the solemn
conclusion that we are now on the margin of
the end of this age and dispensation.   Nor
does the Great Pyramid fail to tell us the same
thing. Measuring off one thousand eight hundred and seventy-seven inches from the beginning of the Grand Gallery for the one thousand
eight hundred and seventy-seven years since
the birth of Christ, there remain but a few
inches more to bring us to its end.   So likewise
when we go forward on the dial of the precessional cycle to observe the condition of the
heavens when the last of these inches is
counted off, the astronomical indications are
correspondingly remarkable.   The Pleiades
which were on the meridian when the Pyra-

mid was built are then far to the east, with the
vernal equinox at the same time precisely the
same distance from that meridian to the west,
whilst the distance from one to the other
measures the exact age of the Pyramid at that
date.   At the same time *a* Draconis will again
be on the meridian below the pole, but then
just seven times lower than at the time of the
Pyramid's building.   This final downward-
ness of seven times is strikingly suggestive of
the Dragon's complete dethronement.   And
what is still more remarkable, whilst *a* Draconis is on the meridian at this low point,
Aries, the Ram, appears on the meridian
above, with the line passing exactly through
his horns !   A more vivid astronomical sign
of the overthrow of Satan under the dominion
of the Prince of the flock of God it is not possible to conceive.   It is as if the very heavens
were proclaiming that then the ever-living
Lamb takes to him his great power, and enters
upon his glorious reign !

The Pyramid and the Jew.

It is the opinion of many earnest believers
in the Scriptures that God is not yet done with
the Jews as a distinct and peculiar people.   As
a nation they rejected Christ and fell from

their high pre-eminence, and are now on precisely the same footing with the Gentiles with
regard to the Christian dispensation. There
is no way of salvation nor any special privi-
leges for them now other than the Gospel
offers to all men alike. Through the atone-
ment of Christ and union with him, there is
redemption for their souls the same as others,
but in no other way. But the belief of many
is that they are preserved in their singular
distinctness, even in unbelief, as the subject
of a grand restoration and conversion when
the times of the Gentiles are fulfilled, and
that blindness in part has happened unto them,
in which as a people they will remain till the
time of the revelation of Jesus Christ at his
second coming. And to this belief the Great
Pyramid would also seem to answer in a very
marked manner.

. A special national token of the Jew is the
sabbatic system. It was given of God, and
made to pervade the whole Jewish economy
as a thing by which the chosen people were to
be distinguished from all other nations, and in
the observance of which they were to exhibit
themselves as God's people. Disregard of this
was held to be treason to their King, and a
forfeiture of all their rights to the promises

And this sabbatic system is specially characteristic of the so-called Queen's Chamber and
the horizontal passage leading to it.

They reached their highest point when of
them Christ was born. The same unbelief by
which they then were broken off they have
ever since retained. Hence the avenue which
I take as a symbol of their history from Christ's
time is horizontal, except that the last seventh
of it drops lower than any other part. If the
latter chapters of Ezekiel (from the thirty-
sixth onward) and many other passages are to
be literally taken, and there is great difficulty
in understanding them in any other way, there
is to come for Israel a grander restoration than
that of their return from Babylon, when they
will be re-established in holiness according to
their ancient estate, and all their early institutes again be righted up and put into full
effect. Hence this low horizontal passage terminates in a grand sabbatic room full of the
most important notations of the measures and
proportions of the whole Pyramid.

Those who hold to this restoration of the
Jews hold also that they will be returned in
their present unbelief and blindness as regards
the true Messiah, and will only afterwards
have the scales removed from their eyes after

the manner of Paul, who in this respect was as one born *before the time*. And this also would seem to be distinctly set forth. Two ventilating tubes have recently been discovered in the so-called Queen's Chamber, which the builders left entirely closed over with a thin unbroken scale, which not only shut them from all observation but rendered them of no practical effect whatever. The room has therefore always been noted for its foul air and noisome smell, for the atmosphere there was left without circulation for four thousand years. These tubes extended inward through the masonry and into the stones forming the walls of the room, all nicely cut, but for about one inch they were not cut through into the room itself. On the hidden sides of the walls these air-channels were open, but on the visible sides within the room the surface was smooth, even, and unbroken, the same as any other part. It was only by something of an accident that these scales were broken and the channels opened into the room itself. So singular an arrangement could have none other than a symbolic intent. No architectural reason for the peculiarity can at all be traced. And most strikingly would it serve to signify the blindness of the Jew. and his deadness in unbelief, needing only the breaking away of those scales for the free breath of God to purify everything again. And if this is the meaning of the symbol, it accords precisely with the idea of the re-establishment of the Jewish nationality before the great conversion, and that this breaking away of the disabling and defiling scales of blindness and unbelief remains to be accomplished after entrance upon the state symbolized by this room. And even then it is only removed by a breakage and violence entirely distinct from the ordinary course of things, which would also be fulfilled in case the general conversion of the Jews is to be brought about after the manner of that type of it exhibited in Paul, who was converted as no other man ever has been by the personal apocalypse of the Lord Jesus.

It is also fully agreed by those who hold to the belief of a restoration of the Jews, that they will then be lifted spiritually far above the dead level which has characterized them as a nation since the fall of Jerusalem, and that quite a new, higher, and holier spirit than they ever experienced before will then be breathed into their ancient ceremonial. And the same would seem to be symbolized in this chamber. It has no proper floor, and is entered from a very low plane, even lower than the avenue in general. But inside there is a base-line marked evenly around it at a range with the square top of the entrance passage, indicating a grand lifting up after having entered. It is in the relative spaces above this line that the sabbatism and exalted proportions and commensurations of the apartment appear.

This opens an entirely new field in pyramid interpretations, which calls for a more enlarged and thorough examination. But what does that horizontal sabbatic passage, starting from the level of Christ's death and dropping lower in the last seventh of its floorline, mean, if not the Jew who has risen no higher since the rejection of his Messiah, but has fallen lower of late by his rationalism, though still preserving his distinctness from all other peoples? What can that remarkable, separate, sabbatic room mean, if not intended to set forth a separate and peculiar earthly destiny of the Jew? And what can that grand uplifting and the breaking through of those thin stoppages of the ventilation signify, if not the re-quickening by the Spirit of God which is promised to the Jew for the sake of his fathers, when once he shall look upon him whom he has pierced?

The Pyramid and Heaven.

The crown of Christian theology and hope is the doctrine concerning heaven, the residence of God and his glorified people. When the Saviour left the earth, he said, "I go to prepare a place for you." Abraham looked for a permanent city. Paul spoke hopefully of "a building of God, a house not made with hands, eternal in the heavens." John beheld and wrote of "that great city, the holy Jerusalem," even "Jerusalem the golden," of which the Church ever sings with such fondness and delight. And this too is symbolized in the Great Pyramid. If nothing else, the granite chamber in which the dispensations of this world terminate may serve to tell of it. But that chamber seems rather to relate to the consummated earthly than to the heavenly. There is reason to believe that another and superior chamber exists in the mighty edifice, more fully answering to the celestial city. The sabbatic chamber is on the twenty-fifth course of the masonry, and the granite chamber on the fiftieth. To make up the complete count there would have to be a third on the one hundredth course, corresponding to "the third heaven." The Apocalypse, that book of the consummations, seems also to call for such a chamber. As "the seven churches" under "the seven stars" are found in the Grand Gallery, and the judgment dispensation in the ante-room leading to the granite chamber, and "the great tribulation" in the granite blocks which hang over the passage-way through that ante-room, there would need to be another and higher apartment to answer to the heavenly Jerusalem, which the Apocalypse introduces as the crown of all. The piles of ancient rubbish from the building of this pyramid which cover the breast of the hill also add their indications of another chamber of grander materials than the others, and higher up in the edifice. After a rain Prof. Smyth paced about among the gutters which the wash cut into these piles of chips and splinters of stone, to see what he could find. "Towards the top of the heap and just in front of, though at a great distance from, the Pyramid's entrance portal," he found "frequent splinters and fragments of green and white *diorite*." This is a compact, very hard, crypto-crystalline formation, whitish, speckled with black or greenish-black. It is the material of which the celebrated stone statue now in the Boolak Museum is cut. It is not native to the pyramid region, and could only have been brought there from far, whilst the number of these spalls and fragments intermixed with the earth and other chippings and offal in the process of this pyramid's building would indicate some extensive use of that excellent material in this structure. Their occurrence near the top of the furthest distance of these piles from the Pyramid would show that the use made of this rock was high up in the edifice and toward its completion. But in none of the present openings has anything been found made of diorite, or anything like it. Therefore, Prof. Smyth, in debating over these fragments, says, " I was compelled to gaze up at the Pyramid with its vast bulk, and believe that there is another chamber still undiscovered there, and one which will prove to be the very muniment room of the whole monument."*

And even the way to it may perhaps be found from a suggestion which I draw from the Apocalypse. The numberless multitude before the throne of God (chap. 7 : 9–17) comes " *out of* the great tribulation," and if those granite blocks suspended over the way through the ante-room to the King's Chamber denote the great tribulation, as they so expressively do,

---

* Life and Work, pp. 187, 188.

the way to a room symbolic of heaven would seem to be directly from those blocks, just where nobody has ever searched for it. Those blocks hang in grooves, and have a boss or knob left on the side as if meant to be slid up for a purpose; and the vision of John would seem to imply that the lifting of them would uncover the way to the room which would be the symbol of glory. A light bore with a rod so directed as to strike behind those blocks would probably reveal whether or not there is such a passage from either side at that point. And until the facts are ascertained by adequate examination, I am inclined to believe, from general analogy and from the correspondence in all other points with the Bible, and especially with the Apocalyptic outlines, that behind those blocks will be found the way to another and superior chamber, situated in the upper centre of the building on the one hundredth course of the masonry. I also anticipate that when it is discovered it will present an exact square, sixteen pyramid cubits every way, with perhaps three distinct entrances on each side, and answering in its prophetic readings to the twenty-first chapter of the Book of the Revelation. Of course this is only a hypothesis, a theoretic persuasion which needs to be tested by further explorations, but it rests on considerations sufficiently strong to beget in me the belief that it will be verified in fact. Hence I have had the place and proportions of such a room indicated on the diagram.

THE PYRAMID AND THE SPIRITUAL UNIVERSE.

But man is not the only rational creature God has made. As the interval below, between him and nothing, is filled up with uncounted orders and forms of being, so on rational as well as Scriptural grounds it is part of our common faith that there are many intellectual and spiritual orders above, between him and the infinite Creator. These rank in series over series of angels and archangels, seraphim and cherubim, principalities and powers. And as the Pyramid is a Scriptural image of the Church, so it is also of this whole spiritual universe. Galloway, in his *Egypt's Record of Time*, has noted that " the ascending scale of natures above man was revealed to Jacob in vision. The collective nature of man is, as it were, at the basis of a mighty pyramid of spiritual natures ascending by successive stages to one glorious apex, from which the whole derives unity, from which the whole has pro-

ceeded, and on which it depends for existence.
This glorious spiritual pyramid appears to be
that which was revealed to Jacob at Bethel,
when a solitary traveller on his way to Padan
Aram : a mighty ladder or scale of being ascending from man to the highest heaven; a
sublime idea of the spiritual universe proceed-
ing from one, and built up into one glorious
head, a world not of gross and dead materials,
but of living spirit and flame, full of the
adoring love and active service of God, at the
summit of which the presence of Jehovah was
beheld revealed " (pp. 339, 340).   And this
grand, striking, and truthful conception of the
universe bound together and headed up in One
supreme original of all, we have here in material form, consolidated in stone, worthy in
some measure too of the eternal vastness and
magnificence of the subject.

Thus then the Great Pyramid answers
throughout to all history and all Revelation.
The substance of both Testaments and all the
dispensations of God toward man are here
traced in unchanging rock, more than five
centuries before Moses.   How came these
things into this pile, and nowhere else on earth
but in the Bible ?   Whence came this sublime
science before the days of science,—this knowl-

edge of all history then only in its beginnings,—
this understanding of all sacred doctrines and
prophecies before all other existing records of
them? By what marvellous eccentricities of
chance originated these monumental prophecies, this prehistoric picturing of coming ages,
these symbolizations of the mysterious Providence of God toward our world for four thousand years, this fore-announcement of the end
from the beginning, this sublime petrifaction
of the divine word ere ever a chapter of it
was traced in our Scriptures? When we find
these things in the Bible written long afterwards we call them *inspired*. What then shall
we call them when we find them all securely
laid up in stone hundreds and thousands of
years anterior to that Holy Book, and now
opened to us with superadded marvels upon
which the Bible scarcely touches? I know
not how others may be impressed, but I feel
as if I would be shutting my eyes to truth,
suppressing the force of evidence, and with-
standing demonstration, did I not joyfully
admit and embrace the fact that we have here
a precious memorial from the same blessed
Jehovah from whom we have our glorious
Bible, erected by some chosen people whom his
own Spirit guided, and at the same time a most

ancient monumental witness to all the holy truths and histories.

And yet the subject is not exhausted. There are various other interesting matters to be considered, all tending to the same conclusion; but I cannot enter upon them now. Reluctantly, I must close again without reaching the end of what needs to be said in a proper presentation of the case. Only one little item more, which seems to belong here, will I yet notice, and with that I conclude this lecture.

The Pyramid and Jerusalem.

If this Pyramid is what it would thus seem to be, it would be natural to infer that it ought to have some connection with or reference to Jerusalem. All the institutes and revelations of God had their chief centre there for more than a thousand years. God made it his own sacred metropolis, the only one he ever had localized upon earth. There his only temple stood. There his holy law was deposited. Thither his people were required to come for the celebration of their most distinguishing services. There was the royal seat of his chosen kings. There was the sacred capitol of his consecrated priests, of his inspired prophets, of his holy scribes. There the glorious

Messiah presented himself to the elect nation.
There he died for the sins of the world. There
he rose triumphant from the dead. There he
ascended into heaven. There he poured out
the Holy Ghost. There he inaugurated the
Christian Church. There he sent forth his
inspired apostles for the conquest of the world
to the religion of the cross. Nay, there he is
to appear again when he comes the second
time as he has promised. And if the Great
Pyramid belongs at all to the great system of
God's redemptive interpositions it could hardly
be wanting in some reference to that "city of
the Lord, the Zion of the Holy One of Israel."
So at least it appeared to me, and led me to
search for the missing indications. I knew
that the Pyramid's most distinguished cubit
answers to the sacred cubit of Moses; that
the capacity measure of the Pyramid's granite
Coffer is the same as that of the Ark of the
Covenant; that the sabbatic system of the
Jews is distinctly noted in connection with the
Queen's Chamber; and that the molten sea
had proportions of earth-commensuration which
also appear in the size of the Pyramid's main
chamber. These are indeed remarkable and
significant coincidences, but they do not give so
direct a reference as I thought ought to exist.

It hence occurred to me to ascertain the exact direction of Jerusalem from the Great Pyramid and to try whether it would fit to any of its interior angles.   Having used two different maps to make sure of accuracy, the result came out exactly the same in both, namely, that three of the main inside angles of the Great Pyramid applied to its north side eastward, point directly to Jerusalem ! If a cannon-ball were shot from the Great Pyramid's north side at the precise angle eastward as that of the entrance passage computed with the base-line, or that of the main ascending passage computed with the same line, or that of the Grand Gallery computed with the passage to the Queen's Chamber, that ball, could it reach so far, would strike the Holy City !

Of itself this might be passed as of no special significance, but taken in connection with what has been developed in this lecture, the unexpected discovery induced a feeling as if the half-smothered pile with all its burden of centuries suddenly arose out of its sands and rubbish, lifted up its stony hand, and looking the very image of old time, pointed its heavy and half pendent finger to the city of Melchisedek, David, and Solomon, saying as with a voice out of the bottom ages, "Look over there! Savants of the earth, and all ye that inquire, go yonder! There observe, listen, and wait, and ye shall know whence I am, and whereof I witness!"

" And I heard a loud voice saying in Heaven, Now is come salvation, and strength, and the kingdom of our God, and the power of His Christ: for the accuser of our brethren is cast down, which accused them before our God day and night.

" And they overcame him by the blood of the Lamb, and by the word of His testimony."—REV. 12 : 10, 11.

Lecture Third.

WHATEVER may be ultimately concluded respecting the origin and intent of the Great Pyramid, it is
certainly one of the most astonishing works ever produced by man. Apart from
all else, the coincidences between it and our
most advanced physical sciences, together with
the thorough correspondence between it and
the Scriptures, as pointed out in preceding
lectures, establishes for it a wonderfulness if
not a sacredness unequalled by anything outside the sphere of miracle. But the history
of traditions and opinions concerning it is
quite as remarkable as itself, and also strongly
confirmatory of the conclusions towards which
we have been advancing. To show this and
to indicate some of the attendant results is
what I propose in the present lecture.

It is a singular fact and not without significance that whilst this oldest, largest and highest edifice of stone ever piled by human hands

(171)

has been before the eyes of the most intelligent portions of the race for more than four thousand years, the learned world has not yet been able to settle what to think of it. Strange to say, it has always been a puzzle and a mystery.

THE ANCIENT TRADITIONS.

The Jews up to the Saviour's time had a cherished tradition that this Pyramid was built before the flood. Josephus, the learned scribe, gives it as historic fact that Seth and his immediate descendants " were the inventors of that peculiar sort of wisdom which is concerned with the heavenly bodies and their order. And that their inventions might not be lost before they were sufficiently known, upon Adam's prediction that the world was to be destroyed, they made two pillars, the one of brick, the other of stone. They inscribed their discoveries on them both, that in case the pillar of brick should be destroyed by the flood, the pillar of stone might remain and exhibit these discoveries to mankind." He also adds, " Now this (pillar) remains in the land of Siriad (Egypt) to this day." (*Jewish Antiquities*, i, 2.) Such an idea so strongly rooted in the mind of God's chosen people is very noteworthy, to say the least.

The Arabians had a corresponding tradition. In a manuscript (preserved in the Bodleian Library, and translated by Dr. Sprenger) Abou Balkhi says, " The wise men previous to the flood, foreseeing an impending judgment from heaven, either by submersion or by fire, which would destroy every created thing, built upon the tops of the mountains in Upper Egypt many pyramids of stone, in order to have some refuge against the approaching calamity. Two of these buildings exceeded the rest in height, being four hundred cubits high, and as many broad, and as many long. They were built with large blocks of marble, and they were so well put together that the joints were scarcely perceptible. Upon the exterior of the building every charm and wonder of physic was inscribed."

Massoudi, another Arab writer, gives the same even more circumstantially, and says that on the eastern or Great Pyramid as built by these ancients the heavenly spheres were inscribed, " likewise the positions of the stars and their circles, together with the history and chronicles of time past, of that which is to come, and of every future event."

Another Arabic fragment, claiming to be a translation from an ancient Coptic papyrus, gives a similar account of the origin of the pyramids, and states that "innumerable precious things" were treasured in these buildings, including "the mysteries of science, astronomy, geometry, physic, and much useful knowledge."

So, too, the famous traveller, Ibn Batuta, says, that "the pyramids were constructed by Hermes, the same person as Enoch and Edris, to preserve the arts and sciences and other intelligence during the flood." And it was by reason of fanciful exaggerations of this same tradition that Al Mamoun made his forced entrance into this edifice.

Of course these accounts cannot be accepted in their literal terms. They are manifestly at fault in various particulars. The very oldest of the pyramids, by its own testimony, was not built till six hundred years after the flood. Seth and Enoch therefore were not its builders, whatever they may have contributed indirectly to it. Nor was the motive for it just the one alleged, though perhaps involving something of the truth. The idea of the storage of material treasures, or of literal inscriptions on the walls and stones, has also been proven erroneous, at least as to what now remains of the edifice. But where so much smoke is there is

apt to be some fire.   Nearly every superstition
in the world has some truth at the bottom by
which it was brought into being, and there is
every probability that there is here also some
kernel of reality.   The pyramids certainly
exist, and they exist just where these traditions locate them.   The great one also proves
itself possessed of a marked scientific character.   Much of this science must necessarily
have come over from antediluvian times.   Six
hundred years were too short for mankind to
have made all the observations here recorded.
Noah had special revelations in the science of
measures, mechanics, and all that superior
wisdom necessary for the building of a ship
larger than the Great Eastern, and capable of
weathering a wilder and wider sea than ever
was navigated before or since.   What he and
his fathers knew before the flood he certainly
would not leave behind when he embarked
for a new world, which it was his conscious
mission to people.   The implements used in
the building of the ark, the knowledge of
their uses, and how to manufacture them, together with all that God had taught or man
had learned on the other side of the flood, he
took with him into the ark, and with the same
disembarked on our side of that awful water.

By some of his immediate descendants only a short time after the death, if not within the lifetime of his son Shem, the Great Pyramid was built. Of necessity, therefore, the science by which and to which this pyramid was fashioned, and perhaps the very tools which helped to build the ark, at least the knowledge of how to make and use such tools, came over from beyond the flood, and found imperishable memorial in this monument. Hence, though not built by Seth and the Sethite antediluvian patriarchs, there was still a real connection between it and them—between their science and what it embodies.

And even what these traditions state with regard to the intent of the building is not wholly without basis in reason. It is pretty clear that there was an atheistic and God-defiant science before the flood the same as now, which would necessarily create anxiety on the part of the holy patriarchs to preserve and perpetuate the pure truth as God had given it. Their religious fidelity would involve this, and we know that they were faithful in this respect. As a false worship, an oppressive rule, a corrupt system of weights and measures, and a perverted life in general were set up by Cain and his wicked seed, luring the world to destruction, Seth and his posterity, as they "continued to esteem God as the Lord of the universe and to have an entire regard to virtue," held to another theology, science, and system of things very sacred and dear to them, which they would be most religiously concerned to preserve and transmit to remotest generations. Noah as a faithful Sethite would be specially anxious and diligent to inculcate and perpetuate that order, his faithfulness to which had saved him and his house when all the rest of mankind perished. The faithful among his descendants could not but share in the same anxieties, particularly when they saw mankind again relapsing into the old Cainite apostasy. Out of devotion to the truth of God, nothing could be more natural for them than, over against the impious Babel tower, to wish for some permanent memorial to God and the sacred wisdom and teaching which they had from him. Acting thus under the holiest of impulses, especially if aided in it by divine inspiration, as Noah was in the building of the ark, just such a modest but mighty science-laden pillar as the Great Pyramid might be anticipated as the result, and the essential import of these strange traditions thus be realized.

MORE MODERN OPINIONS.

But over against all such ideas there is a long array of the most diverse and contradictory opinions.

For a long time it has been customary to regard the pyramids as mere monuments of the power and folly of the monarchs by whom they were erected, and of the enslavement of their subjects. Pliny says that they were built for ostentation and to keep an idle people at work. Hales calls them "stupendous monuments of ancient ostentation and tyranny." F. Barham Zincke enlarged on the theory that "capital is bottled-up labor, convertible again at pleasure into labor or the produce of labor;" that as there were no government bonds, consols, and productive stocks in which to invest in the time of the pyramid builders, they might as well invest their barren surplusage in making for themselves eternal monuments, or some safe and magnificent abodes for their mummies, as to conceal it in barren treasuries to tempt other people's covetousness; and that this is the way to account for the pyramids! Robinson refers to them as "probably the earliest as well as the loftiest and most vast of all existing works of man upon the face

of the earth," but thinks "there is little room
to doubt that they were erected chiefly if not
solely from the vain pride of human pomp and
power." Stanley speaks of them as the pro-
duct of a silly ambition, the study of which
can make them only "more definite objects of
contempt." To such an estimate Brande has
sufficiently answered that "this is a very superficial and prejudiced view of the matter. The
varying magnitude of the pyramids, the fact
of their being scattered over a space extending
lengthwise about seventy miles, and their extraordinary number, appear to show pretty
conclusively that they must have been constructed (in their original, at least) from a sense
of utility and duty, and not out of caprice or
from a vain desire to perpetuate the names or
the celebrity of their founders."

Some trace the pyramids to Nimrod, and
think they were meant to be towers of security. But the idea of a Nimrodic origin of
these structures is a mere surmise, wild and
without a particle of evidence looking in that
direction. And as retreats for men in case of
flood or invasion, no such structures ever could
have been thought of by any rational people,
and none others could have built them. Destitute of habitable space within, incapable in

their perfect state of being ascended, and furnishing neither standing room nor shelter on
their summits, they would be a poor resort for
safety in any such emergency.

Mandeville considered them the granaries
built by Joseph to store up the products of
the seven years of fatness against the succeed-
ing seven years of famine.   But nothing could
be more ill adapted for a purpose of that sort.
They were a thousand times more costly than
the worth of all the corn they could hold, and
any one of them would require more time to
construct than double the number of years
Joseph had to prepare for the famine.   We
also have the highest evidence now that the
Great Pyramid, which alone was capable of
serving in this line, was built hundreds of years
before Joseph was born.

Others have regarded them as astronomical
observatories, and some have even figured an
imaginary base around each where the stu-
dents of the sky might sit and contemplate
like great heavenly choirs.   But that such
amazing buildings all in one low place and incapable of being ascended should have been
erected merely to furnish sittings for a few
star-gazers, for whom any rock or hillock would
answer as well, is a little too much for credulity

itself. And the modern uncovering of the Great Pyramid's finish at the base has effectually dispersed forever all these imaginary choirs.

Others have supposed the pyramids intended as artificial barricades against the sands of the desert or the breaking forth of the Nile. But the eye of an observer sees at a glance the paltry absurdity of such an idea. The Nile never had any notion of breaking over this hill of solid rock, and if it had the pyramids were a vain thing to hinder either it or the sands of the desert.

THE TOMB THEORY.

A more extensively accepted opinion now is that the pyramids were all designed for royal sepulchres "and nothing else," which is doubtless true of most of them. It is possible also that the idea of a tomb for Cheops may have mingled with the original design of the first and greatest of them, though there is no evidence to that effect. It may have been given out for a tomb for him as a mere blind to the nation at large, but in any event the tomb idea never could have been more than subordinate and incidental.

We know now that this pyramid was built

during the reign of Cheops, in the so-called
Fourth Dynasty of Egyptian Kings. But it
is nearly as certain that Cheops never was entombed in it. The account given by Herodotus is sometimes quoted in proof that he was,
but it is clearly a misunderstanding. That
account says that Cheops was buried in some
subterraneous place where "the Nile water introduced through an artificial duct surrounds
an island." But there is not a single opening
either in or under the Great Pyramid which is
not far above the highest Nile level. That
Cheops never was entombed in the so-called
King's Chamber is therefore certain in so far
as what Herodotus tells about it is accepted.
Personally he knew nothing. He only records
what was told him. And the priest from whom
he got his statement either was as ignorant as
himself, or Cheops never was buried in this
pyramid. Diodorus says positively that Cheops
was not buried here, but in some obscure and
unknown place. For six hundred years after
Al Mamoun broke open this pyramid the
Arab writers who tell of the feat, say not a
word of any human remains or indications of
sepulture being found. Shehab Eddin Amed
Ben Yahiya, on the contrary, says that "nothing
was discovered as to the motive or time of its

construction." Massoudi tells of certain find-
ings, such as colored magic stones, columns of
gold which nobody could move, images in
green stone, and a cock with flaming eyes,
which stories none but a Moslem can believe;
but says not a word of the finding of any man
or any evidence of the use of the place as a
tomb. And not less than a dozen of the best
European authors on the subject, from Helfricus to Sir Gardiner Wilkinson's Guide Book
to Modern Egypt, though some of them believe
that the Great Pyramid was intended for a
sepulchral monument, agree in stating that
there is no proof that anybody ever was entombed in it.[*]

---

[*] Helfricus (1565) and Baumgarten (1594) considered the
Great Pyramid a tomb, but held that no one was ever buried
in it. Pietro Della Valle (1616), Thevenot (1655), and Maillet
(1692) give it as the common belief that no one ever was therein
entombed. Vausleb (1664) could find no clue by which to determine why this pyramid was built. Shaw (1721) denies that
it ever was a tomb or ever was intended to be one. Jomard
(1801), having studied all the features of this edifice, and compared them day by day with all the facts and forms of old
Egyptian pyramids, wrote concerning it, " Everything is mysterious, I repeat it, in the construction and distribution of this
monument, the passages oblique, horizontal, sharply bent, of
different dimensions!" " We are not at all enlightened either
upon the origin or the employment, the utility or any motive
whatever for the Grand Gallery and various passages." Sir G.
Wilkinson says, " It may be doubted whether the body of the
king was really deposited in the sarcophagus," as he calls it.

But if this edifice was reared to be a royal sepulchre, why was it not used as such ? Very curious are the explanations to which the tomb theorists háve resorted to account for the failure. Diodorus among the old writers, and Baumgarten among the more modern ones, say, that the people of Egypt were so enraged at the sufferings endured from the builders of the two greatest pyramids, and at their various violent actions, as to threaten to tear them out of their sepulchres, whereupon "they both charged their relatives at their death to inter them secretly in some obscure place." To this Colonel Vyse has conclusively answered, " If Cheops reigned fifty years, and had sufficient power to construct the Great Pyramid, it can scarcely be supposed that his body was not deposited in it [if so intended], particularly as his successor is said to have reigned fifty-six years, and to have erected a similar tomb for himself, which he could scarcely have done had his predecessor's tomb been violated or any doubt have existed about the security of his own."

Helfricus and Veryard get over the difficulty

And Mr. St. John does not consider the Coffer a sarcophagus at all, and thinks the Great Pyramid never was and never was meant to be a tomb.

by assigning the Great Pyramid to that Pharaoh who perished in the Red Sea while pursuing the departing children of Israel. As that monarch's body was never recovered, they say of course his sepulchre never was used! Still others explain that the tomb was Joseph's, and became vacant at the time of the Exodus, as his brethren took his body with them when they went up to the land of promise. But unfortunately for these explanations, the Great Pyramid was built some six hundred years before Moses and several hundred years before the viceroyalty of Joseph.

The truth is that the tomb theory does not fit the facts, the traditions, or any knowledge that we have on the subject. It is wholly borrowed from the numerous later pyramids, ambitiously and ignorantly copied after it, which *were* intended and used for royal sepulchres, but with which the Great Pyramid has nothing in common, save locality and general shape. In all the examination to which it has been subjected, whether in ancient or modern times, and in all the historic fragments concerning it, there is nothing whatever to give or to bear out the idea that its intention was simply that of a royal sepulchral monument, or that can legitimately raise the tomb theory any higher than a possible but very improbable *supposition*.

SOMETHING MORE THAN A TOMB.

It is also important in this connection to note that something wholly distinct from a mere sepulchre, or something additional and of much greater significance, has always haunted the convictions of those who have most profoundly studied this wonderful structure.

Sandys gives place to the idea of a tomb, but considers it a tomb built with special reference to the symbolization of spiritual doctrines and hopes, together with "conceits from astronomical demonstrations." Greaves accepts it for a tomb, but one framed with intent to represent spiritual ideas. Shaw denies its tombic character altogether, and pronounces it a temple of religious mysteries. Perry admits that it may have served as a royal tomb, but had special reference to sacred beliefs. Jomard gave but little credit to the treasure theory of the East or the tomb theory of the West, and considered this pyramid likely to prove itself gifted with something of great value to the civilized world, particularly in the matter of measures and weights. Wilkinson considers

the pyramids tombs, but is persuaded that some
were "intended for astronomical purposes."
Mr. St. John holds them as meant for religious uses and symbolisms. Agnew takes them
as tombs, but at the same time as embodiments
of science—"emblems of the sacred sphere,
exhibited in the most convenient architectural
form"—a squaring of the circle outside (which
is true only of the Great Pyramid) and a
setting forth of various geometric, astronomic,
and mathematical mysteries inside. Sir Isaac
Newton considered them sources of very important information on the subject of measures.
Sir John Herschel was persuaded of the Great
Pyramid's astronomical character, and found
in it standards of measure which he urged
England to adopt in preference to any other
on earth. Beckett Denison admits it to be a
highly scientific monument of metrology,
mathematics, and astronomy. Hekekyan Bey,
of Constantinople, in a volume published in
1863, ignores the idea of the granite Coffer
being a sarcophagus, and speaks of it as "the
king's stone," deposited in its sanctuary as a
record of a standard of measure. Proctor
argues that it is "highly probable" that the
builders of the Great Pyramid sought "to represent symbolically in the proportions of the

building such mathematical and astronomical relations as they were acquainted with," and "may have had a quasi scientific desire to make a lasting record of their discoveries, and of the collected knowledge of their time." And since what has been written and pointed out by John Taylor, Piazzi Smyth, Sir John Vincent Day, Rev. T. Goodsir, Captain B. F. Tracy, Mr. James Simpson, Henry Mitchell, Dr. Alexander Mackey, Charles Casey, Rev. F. R. A. Glover, Hamilton Smith, J. Ralston Skinner, and others, within the last fifteen years, we can but wonder that any one at all read up on the subject should think of withholding from this colossal monument the award of something vastly more than a mere tomb.

That subterranean chamber cut deep into the solid rock would seem to indicate a tomb, but that chamber never was finished, and no one pretends that it was ever used for sepulture. It must have been meant for some other purpose. A vast tumulus, solidly built, with but few and narrow openings, terminating in finely polished rooms in its interior, would seem to agree with the idea of a grand sepulchre, but when we find in it a transcendent geodesic plan of location, equally dividing the

earth surface between the equator and the
north pole, palpably marking the centre of all
habitable land distribution on the globe, and
giving the best meridional line for the zero of
latitude for all nations, surely we ought to
begin to think of something else. A square
with four sloping sides built up to a point in
the centre, would seem to be a proper device
for an enduring royal mausoleum, and hence
the same was long accepted in Egypt for sepulchral monuments of the kings, but when we
find in the first and original of them a perfect
geometric figure, so framed that the four sides
of its base bear the same proportion to its vertical height as the circumference of a circle to
its radius, that each of its base-lines measures
the even ten millionth part of the semi-axis
of the earth just as many times as there are
days in the year, that its height multiplied by
10^9 gives the mean distance between the earth
and its great centre of light, that its unit of
length is the even five hundred millionth part
of the polar diameter of the globe we inhabit,
that its two diagonals of base measure in
inches the precise number of years in the great
precessional cycle, that its bulk of masonry is
an even proportion of the weight of the earth
itself, and that its setting and shaping are

squared and oriented with microscopic accuracy,—nothing of which is to be found in the scores of neighboring pyramidal tombs,—by what law of right reason are we to dismiss from our thoughts every idea but that of a mere sepulchre? A polished stone coffer, conveniently deep, and wide, and long to accommodate the body of a man, and put up in noble place as here, would seem to bespeak a royal sarcophagus, but when we find that Coffer of the utmost plebeian plainness, quite disproportioned to such a purpose, devoid of all known covering, ornament, inscription or sepulchral insignia, incapable of being placed in its chamber with a body in it, is there not room for rational doubt that it was ever meant or used for a burial casket? And when we perceive in it a most accurately shaped standard of measures and proportions, its sides and bottom cubically identical with its internal space, the length of its two sides to its height as a circle to its diameter, its exterior volume just twice the dimensions of its bottom, and its whole measure just the fiftieth part of the chamber in which it was put when the edifice was built, we may well wonder what all such unparalleled scientific elaborations have to do with a mere tomb! The inclined entrance

of a fitting size to receive a coffin, and down
which a coffin could be conveniently slid to
some chamber in the depths below, would be
in keeping with a tombic intent, but when we
find it terminating below in what never was a
burial-chamber, and turned above in a sharp
angle which no coffin such as the Coffer could
pass, and that entrance most inconveniently
located just to bring it into the plane of the
meridian at an angle to point to the lower culmination of a pole star at the same time that
the Pleiades are on the meridian above,—does
it not become necessary to think of something
more than a mere tomb, if not to abandon that
idea altogether ?   All the other pyramids of
Egypt were meant for tombs, but none of them
have any upward passages or upper chambers.
The Grand Gallery in this edifice, so sublime
in height, so abrupt in beginning and termination, so different from all the other passages
before or beyond it, so elaborately and peculiarly contrived and finished in every part, is absolutely incomprehensible on the tomb theory
or on any other, save that of a high astronomical, historical, and spiritual symbolism, having
nothing whatever to do with the entombment
of an Egyptian despot.   And when we find in
this edifice throughout, one great system of

interrelated numbers, measures, weights, angles, temperatures, degrees, geometric problems, cosmic references, and general geodesy, which modern science has now read and verified from it, reason and truth demand of the teachers of mankind to cease writing that " no other object presented itself to the builder of the Great Pyramid than the preparation of his own tomb."

That all these things should appear in a great metrologic, scientific, and symbolic structure, meant to memorialize the most important features of universal nature, history, and theology, we can easily understand.　But that they should turn up in what was never meant to be anything but a tomb, as Lord Valentia, Shaw, Jomard, and others have submitted, is beyond all rational comprehension or belief. Mere literary Egyptologists, whose world of inquiry is bounded by classic tombs, Siriadic sepulchres, and heathen temples,—a few sneering scientists, who find here an impediment to their atheistic philosophies,—consequential theologues and pedants, who have reached the boundaries of wisdom,—and all the wise owls of stereotyped learning, ensconced in their hollownesses of decay,—may pooh-pooh and hoot, but if this pyramid was meant for a tomb

it is the most wonderful sepulchre ever constructed, the mere accidents of which are ten
thousand-fold more magnificent in wisdom,
interest, and worth to mankind, than all the
tombs and Pharaohs of all the dynasties, and
all their other works besides,—a tomb, too, to
which there has now fortunately come a resurrection morning, second only to that which
split open the rocks of Calvary and demonstrated a glorious immortality for man.

Not a Temple of Idolatry.

Brande has expressed the opinion, that " if
we had sufficient knowledge of antiquity, it
would probably be found that the motives
which led to the construction of the pyramids
were, at bottom, nearly identical with those
which led to the construction of St. Peter's
and St. Paul's, and that they are monuments
of religion and piety, as well as of the power
of the Pharaohs." To whatever extent this
was the fact with regard to the Great Pyramid, there is no evidence that it was built for
an idol temple, whether to Athor, as suggested
by Mr. St. John, or to Cheops, as insinuated by
Mr. Osburn. Certain Eastern peoples may
have made pilgrimages to it, as the Western
people do now, or as the Queen of Sheba came

to hear the wisdom of Solomon. The Egyptians themselves may afterwards have accepted it as " the great temple of Suphis," and even appointed priests for the celebration of his worship in connection with it. But that can be much better explained in other ways than by assuming that Cheops built it either as a tomb for his body or as a temple for the honor of his soul.

Egypt was a hotbed of idolatry from the beginning. Its people began by the worship of heroes and heavenly bodies, and ended in the worship of bulls, and goats, and cats, and crocodiles, and hawks, and beetles. Their false religion was in full sway when Cheops was born. Lepsius tells us that the whole land was full of temples, filled with statues of gods and kings, their walls within and without covered with colored reliefs and hieroglyphics in celebration of the virtues of their hero gods and their divine and ever faultless children. " Nothing, even down to the palette of a scribe, the style with which a lady painted her eyelashes, or a walking stick, was deemed too insignificant to be inscribed with the name of the owner, and a votive dedication of the object to some patron divinity." And yet, here is the Great Pyramid, the largest, finest, and most wonderful edifice in all Egypt, situated in the midst of an endless round of tombs, temples, and monuments, all uniformly loaded down with these idolatrous emblems and inscriptions, and yet in all its thirteen acres of masonry, in all its long avenues, Grand Gallery, and exquisite chambers, in any department or place whatever, there has never been found one ancient inscription, votive record, or the slightest sign or shred of Egypt's idolatry! In the centre of the intensest impurity, the Great Pyramid stands without spot, blemish, or remotest taint of the surrounding flood of abominations,—like the incarnate Son of God, sinless in a world of sinners. And to hold such a monument to be itself a temple of idol worship is like calling Christ a minister of Beelzebub.

Historic Fragments.

Passing then to the historic fragments relating to the subject, we find additional reason for the same conclusions.

It is given as a fact, and specially emphasized, that during the building of the Great Pyramid the government of Egypt was strangely and oppressively adverse to the established idolatry of the nation. Cheops stands charged on all sides as at that particular time very " arrogant towards the gods," having shut up the temples, interdicted the customary worship, cast out the images to be defiled on the highways, and compelled even the priests to labor in the quarries.　Hence the indignant hierophant whom Herodotus consulted, said, " The Egyptians so detest the memory of these kings that they do not much like to mention their names."　It thus appears that Cheops was the positive foe and punisher of idolatry at the time this building was being put up, which fact alone wholly and forever sweeps away all idea of this pillar having been erected for any idol's temple or as a votive offering to any god or gods of the Egyptian Pantheon.

It further appears from these fragments, along with other indications, that after the Great Pyramid was completed, late in his life, Cheops relapsed into the old Egyptian idolatry, became a devotee of the very worship which he had so sternly suppressed, and not only reopened the temples, but actually put forth a book on the gods of his country, which was highly esteemed for ages after.*　How,

---

* See Osburn's *Mon. Hist. of Egypt*, vol. i, p. 277.　Also, Shuckford's *Sac. and Prof. Hist.*, vol. i, p. 157.　Also, Lenormant and Chevallier's *Anc. Hist. of the East*, vol. i, p. 207.

then, did it happen that during the thirty or more years in which the Great Pyramid was building, this man, born and reared in idolatry, and dying a devôt of it, was the suppressor of its temples, the enslaver of its priests, and the defiler of its gods? The answer may perhaps be found in another particular with which these fragments make us acquainted.

During the building of the Great Pyramid there was a noted stranger abiding in Egypt, and keeping himself about the spot where the building was going on. The priest consulted by Herodotus describes him as a shepherd, to whom rather than to Cheops the Egyptians attribute this edifice. The precise words recorded by Herodotus are, "They commonly call the pyramids after *Philition*, a shepherd who at that time fed his flocks about the place." (Rawlinson's *Herodotus*, vol. ii, p. 176.) Here is a most remarkable and significant item of information,—an unknown but conspicuous stranger, possessed of flocks and herds, abides about the locality of the Great Pyramid for all the years it was in building, and is so related to the work that all Egypt for more than seventeen hundred years considered him its real originator and builder, Cheops merely furnishing the site, the workmen, and the

materials. Nor was he some great professional
architect, whom Cheops heard of and sent for
to build him a sepulchre. The account says
he was *a shepherd*—a keeper of flocks—and
hence of an order whose business lay in the
line of keeping sheep, but not in the line of
building pyramids to the order of foreign
kings. He is called *"Philition"* or *Philitis*.
This would seem to imply that he was one of
a peculiar and special religious brotherhood,
or that he was a Philistian,—one who came
from or located in Philistia.

There were several classes of Philistines,
different in religion and race. The Philistines of Jewish times are of unsavory odor.
But it was not so with certain earlier Philistines whom the Scriptures mention with honor
as a people specially favored of Jehovah.
When Israel was on the way to Canaan, in
order to revive their drooping confidence, God
told them of a much earlier people whom he
had in like manner conducted up from Egypt.
He calls them "the Caphtorims which came
out of Caphtor" (Deut. 2 : 23). This Caphtor was the very region of Egypt in which the
Great Pyramid stands, and these Caphtorims
from Caphtor, God elsewhere calls " *the Philistines*," whom *He* "brought up from Caphtor."

(Amos 9 : 7.) So that not only from Herodotus and his informant, but from the Bible itself, we learn of *Philistines* once in the neighborhood of the Great Pyramid, who were the objects of the Divine favor, and whom *God* brought up from thence, as he long afterwards brought up the children of Israel.*

---

* It has been found very difficult to trace the origin and history of this early people. The Philistines of the. time of the Judges, and of David, were a long subsequent people, who do not appear in the settlement of Israel under Joshua. They are not mentioned in any of the assaults and conquests of the Jews on their first arrival. Ewald considers this conclusive against their being inhabitants of Palestine at that time. Still, in the time of Abraham, we read of Philistines in Canaan. (Gen. 21 : 32–34.) Abraham was on friendly terms with them, entered into a covenant of peace with them, and "sojourned many days" with them. They feared and reverenced the true God. (Gen. 21 : 22.) Ewald agrees that their language was Shemitic. They were an organized and powerful people. Their sovereigns had the title of *Abimelech*, a Hebrew word, meaning *Father King*, as the sovereigns of Egypt were all called *Pharaoh*, and the sovereigns of Rome, *Cæsar*. The Caphtor, whence they came, Stark makes the Delta of Egypt, and they themselves some early part of the Hycsos or shepherd kings, known to Egyptian history. Dr. Jamieson says, "There is every reason to believe the sovereigns were connected with the shepherd kings of Lower Egypt, and were far superior in civilization and refinement to the Canaanitish tribes around them." (Com. on Gen. 20 : 2.) The Phœnician traditions say they came from Arabia. They differed from the Egyptians in dress and manners, as proven by the monuments; and also in language, laws, and religion, as justly inferable from the Bible notices of them. The intent of the reference to them in Amos 9 : 7 plainly is to show that Israel was not the only people which

There is also another remarkable fragment bearing on the subject. Manetho, an Egyptian priest and scribe, is quoted by Josephus, and others, as saying, " We had formerly a king whose name was Timaus. In his time it came to pass, I know not how, that the Deity was displeased with us; and there came up from the East in a strange manner men of an ignoble race, who had the confidence to invade our country, and easily subdued it by their power without a battle. And when they had our rulers in their hands they demolished the temples of the gods." (See Cory's *Fragments*, p. 257.) This Timaus of Manetho is doubtless the same person as the Chemmes of

---

had been divinely led from one country to settle in another. R. G. Pool considers the allusion as seeming to imply oppression prior to the migration, but that is not necessarily involved. There is no allusion to deliverance, but simply to a bringing of them thither by special divine direction. Abimelech in Gerar, and Melchisedec in Salem, would seem to be closely related as to religion, language, and race. They were perhaps the representatives of two branches of one and the same people, who came into Palestine at one and the same time, from one and the same place in Egypt, under one and the same motive, close about the time of the completion of the Great Pyramid. There certainly is nothing to disprove this conclusion. The name of Abimelech's general-in-chief, *Phicol*, though made up of Hebrew syllables, is not a Hebrew word, but seems to bear an Egyptian influence in its formation, as Pi-hahiroth, Pi-beseth, Pi-thom. It is most likely a designation of office, bearing traces of some connection with Egypt, but not of it.

Diodorus, the Cheops of Herodotus, and the Chufu or Suphis of the monuments. The description is peculiar, and though tinctured with Egypt's proverbial hatred to this class of shepherds, indicates a wonderful influence won over the king by purely peaceable means, which could hardly have been less than supernatural. Manetho himself refers it to the pleasure and displeasure of the Deity, and further adds, that this people "was styled *Hycsos*, that is, *the shepherd kings*," and that "some say they were Arabians."*

Manetho wrote about three hundred years

---

* Wilford, in his *Asiatic Researches*, vol. iii, p. 225, gives an extract from the Hindoo records which seems to sustain, in some important particulars, this fragment of Manetho. The extract says, that one *Tamo-vatsa*, a child of prayer, wise and devout, prayed for certain successes, and that God granted his requests, and that he came into Egypt with a chosen company, entered it "without any declaration of war, and began to administer justice among the people, to give them a specimen of a good king." This Tamo-vatsa is represented in the account as a king of the powerful people called the *Pali*, *shepherds*, who in ancient times governed the whole country from the Indus to the mouth of the Ganges, and spread themselves, mainly by colonization and commerce, very far through Asia, Africa, and Europe. They colonized the coasts of the Persian Gulf, and the sea-coasts of Arabia, Palestine, and Africa, and were the long-haired people called the Berbers in North Africa. They are likewise called *Palestinæ*, which name has close affinity with the *Philition* of Herodotus. These *Pali* of the Hindoo records are plainly identical with some of the Joktanic peoples. See *infra*.

before Christ, and his statements are somewhat mixed with the history of another set of
shepherd kings of a long-subsequent dynasty,
but the ground of the story belongs to the
period of Cheops and the Great Pyramid, for
it was then that this peaceable control was
obtained over the reigning sovereigns by a
shepherd prince, the temples closed, the gods
destroyed, and the people oppressed with labor
for the government.   Manetho says that these
" Arabians " left Egypt in large numbers, but
instead of going to Arabia, they went up to
" that country now called Judea, and there
built a city and named it Jerusalem."

It would thus appear that the shepherd
prince connected with the building of the
Great Pyramid was from Arabia, and subsequently located in Palestine (Philistia), hence
probably called " *Philition* "—the Philistian.
The connection of him with the building of
Jerusalem is very remarkable, and may serve
to identify him with some Scripture character.
Josephus quotes the passage as referring to the
Jews, but that can hardly be the case.   The
Jews did not originally build Jerusalem.   They
did not even have possession of it till the time
of David, about five hundred years after
the Exodus.   Jerusalem existed, and wore at

least a part of its present name, full a thousand years before David. As early as Abraham's time it was the seat of a great king, to whom Abraham himself paid reverence and tithes, and from whom he accepted blessing and communion, as "priest of the Most High God." With reference to his character and office, the Bible calls him MELCHISEDEC, plainly a descriptive and not a proper name, he being first "king of righteousness, and after that also king of Salem." (Heb. 7 : 1, 2.)

WHO WAS MELCHISEDEC?

An illustrious personage thus breaks upon our notice with all the sudden grandeur of the Great Pyramid itself. Who he was has been something of a question for thousands of years,—a question which perhaps cannot be positively answered. Kohlreiff, in his *Chronologia Sacra* (Hamburg, 1724), as cited by Wolfius, identifies this personage with the patriarch Job. There is also more to sustain this view than any other ever presented.

The time is the same. On general internal evidences, Dr. Owen (in *Theologoumen.*), assigns the Book of Job to the period immediately preceding Abraham. The length of Job's life places him in the pre-Abrahamic age of Serug,

Reu, and Peleg.* He evidently lived before
the Exodus, and before the destruction of
Sodom and Gomorrah, for though the Book of
Job refers to Adam, the fall, and the deluge,
there is no allusion whatever to the awful
disaster to the cities of the plain, the Sinaitic
laws, or any of the miraculous events of
Israelitish history. Such an omission in such
a discussion, in the vicinity of these great

---

* "The lives of mankind were so much shortened ere the days
of Abraham, that though he lived but one hundred and seventy-
five years, yet he is said to have 'died in a good old age, an
old man, and full of years.' Peleg, who was five generations
before Abraham, lived two hundred and thirty-nine years.
Reu, the son of Peleg, lived as many. Serug, the son of Reu,
lived two hundred and thirty. But the lives of their descendants were not so long. The LXX in their translation say that
Job lived in all two hundred and forty or two hundred and
forty-eight years. Nahor, the grandfather of Abraham, lived
but one hundred and forty-eight years. Terah, Abraham's
father, lived two hundred and five. Abraham lived one hundred and seventy-five, Isaac lived one hundred and eighty, and
the lives of their children were shorter. If, therefore, Job
lived two hundred and forty or two hundred and forty-eight
years, he must have been contemporaneous with Peleg, Reu,
or Serug, for men's lives were not extended to so great a length
after their days. He lived one hundred and forty years after
his affliction, and when that affliction came he had seven sons
and three daughters, and all his children seem to have been
grown up and settled in life from the beginning of his misfor-
tunes." His age could not therefore be less than two hundred
years at the least. See Shuckford's *Sac. and Profane History*,
vol. i, p. 263, 264, who also makes Job contemporaneous with
Suphis (Cheops).

occurrences, could not happen if these events had preceded it. Job speaks of the rock yielding him a spring of mineral oil (19 : 6), and such oilsprings there evidently were in the region of Sodom and Gomorrah prior to the great burning of those cities, and the earth under and about them ; but they have never since been found. Moses alludes to the same, but only by way of metaphor drawn from the Book of Job, for no such circumstance ever literally occurred in the history of Israel. Those oilsprings were drained and exhausted when those cities burned. Besides, sundry astronomical calculations made from notices of constellations contained in the Book of Job fix the time of the patriarch's great trial contemporaneous with Melchisedec.*

---

* Four constellations are mentioned together in the Book of Job 9 : 9, and 38 : 31, 32, and in four opposite quarters of the heavens, *Kimah*, the Pleiades in the constellation Taurus ; *Kesil*, the equinoctial *nodus* in Scorpio, the name being perpetuated in the Chaldean Kislev or November ; *Mazzaroth*, Sirius or literally Egypt's star sign ; and *Ish*, Aquarius, who in a manner revenged himself on the sons of men in the deluge. These four are named in their oppositions, and so in Job's day, they correspond to the two equinoctial and the two solstitial constellations. *Kimah* answers to the vernal equinox, *Kesil* to the autumnal, and *Mazzaroth* corresponds to the summer solstice, and *Ish* to the winter solstice. President Goguet, in his *Origin of Laws*, a translation of which was published in Edinburgh, in 1761 (the Paris ed. of 1758), makes the calculation by the

The country of the one is also that of the other. Abraham met Melchisedec in Palestine, but no one claims that he was born and reared there. There were important Shemitic migrations hitherward prior to that of Abraham.† In the *Chronicon Paschale* the tradition

---

precessional cycle, and says that it fixes the epoch of Job's trial in the year 2136 B.C., which would be just thirty-four years after the building of the Great Pyramid. Dr. Brinkley, of Dublin, repeated the calculation, and brought it out somewhere about 2130 B.C. Dr. Hales adopts the calculation by Brinkley, and refers to another calculation on the same data by Ducoutant, in a Thesis published in Paris, in 1765, which gives the same within forty-two years. Such a coincidence, says Wemyss, is very striking, and the argument deduced from it, if well founded, would amount nearly to a demonstration.

† "The primeval Canaanites were of the race of Ham, and no doubt originally spoke a dialect closely akin to the Egyptian, but it is clear that before the coming of Abraham into their country they had by some means become Shemitized, since all the Canaanitish names of the time are palpably Shemitic. Probably the movements from the country about the Persian Gulf, of which the history of Abraham furnishes an instance, had been in progress for some time before he quitted Ur, and an influx of emigrants from that-quarter had made Shemitism already predominant in Syria and Palestine at the date of his arrival "—Rawlinson's *Herodotus*, vol. i, p. 537.

Ewald, in his *Hist. of Israel*, argues to the same effect. He says, " It is clear that there was here a primitive people which once extended over the whole land of the Jordan to the left, and to the Euphrates on the right, and to the Red Sea on the south," and that " these people," who had very largely displaced the old Canaanites in Palestine, " were of Shemitic race."—Vol. i, p. 231.

Hence, as Wilkins observes, Abraham on his arrival found the population consisting, at least in a very large measure, of

is received with strong assurance, that Melchisedec, like Abraham, came from beyond the Jordan. Nor is there any doubt of Job's having come from that same mysterious " East."

In general character and position, Job and Melchisedec appear to be one and the same. Paul calls on his Jewish readers to " consider how great this man (Melchisedec) was," and of Job the sacred record is, " This man was the greatest of all the men of the East." Melchisedec was " priest of the Most High God," and of Job it is written that he sent and offered burnt-offerings for his sons and daughters " continually." Melchisedec was a princely personage—" King of Salem ;" and all agree in assigning a princely rank to Job. It remains a question till now, whether he was not a real " king," many maintaining that he was.

---

tribes with which he would have close affinities of blood and language. Hence, also, we have no hint in the Biblical narrative that points to any difference of language, such as we often have when the Jews came in contact with nations whose speech was really unintelligible to them, as the Egyptians (Psalm 81 : 5, 114 : 1). On the contrary we find Abraham negotiating with the children of Heth, making a treaty with Abimelech, Jacob and his sons communing with the people of Shechem, Israel's spies conversing with the inhabitants of the land, and Solomon corresponding with Hiram, without the slightest reference to the need of any interpreter between them. See Wilkins's *Phœnicia and Israel*, pp. 3–10.

He certainly was at least a great emir. Melchisedec was a worshipper of the one true God, outside of the Abrahamic line, and the same is true of Job. From these and other coincidences it would seem that in Melchisedec, King of Salem, we do really meet the great patriarch of Uz, near the end of those one hundred and forty years of glory which succeeded his sore affliction.

The genealogical tables also supply a name which would seem to indicate the existence of an Arabian Job, who appears at the right time and in the right connections to be this same identical patriarch. In the tenth of Genesis, the sacred historian departs entirely from his usual method, in naming the thirteen sons of Joktan, as if for the special purpose of reaching the last in the list.* He sets down

---

* "The design of Moses after he has completed the narrative of the dispersion of the third and fourth generations of the descendants of Noah, and thus related the ancestry of the chief nations of the world, undoubtedly was to continue the line of Shem to that of Abraham only. All interest in the other patriarchal families appears to have ceased ; he takes no notice of any but that of Joktan. The family of Joktan were not the ancestors of the Messiah ; neither were any of the sons of this patriarch so peculiarly distinguished in the subsequent history of Israel, that the enumeration of their names only might have been anticipated in this genealogy. But nothing is written in the Holy Scriptures without an object, and in the absence of any other object for which Moses deviated from his plan, and

that name as *Job-ab*, which is quite capable of being read *father-Job*, in allusion to some such position and career as that of the great patriarch of Uz, or Melchisedec. Alterations were likewise made in the names of Abraham and Sarah in allusion to their special calling and office. The seventy translators from tradition, most of the Hebrew authors, Origen, the Coptic version of Job, the Greek fathers, and various modern writers, represent *Job-ab* and *Job* as one and the same name. In that case we would here have a Job, a veritable Arabian, a descendant of Eber (through Joktan, as Abraham through Peleg), and hence a true *Hebrew* in the older and wider sense, who answers well to all we know either of Melchisedec or the Uzean patriarch.

From Job we have the most unique and independent book in the sacred canon—the sub-

---

recorded the names of the sons of Joktan only, terminating the list with the name of Job-ab or Job,—I conclude that his design was to tell us that the Job who was the youngest son of Joktan was the Job who lived in the land of Uz, though he was not born there, and who suffered and was tempted as the Book of Job has recorded. The sons of Joktan were enumerated that the name of Job might be placed before the children of Israel as the witness to the truth of those doctrines which their patriarchal ancestors received, which Moses taught, and which the Church of God in all ages has believed."—Dr. Townsend's Bible, vol. i, p. 131.

limest section of the inspired records,—a grand
monument. of patriarchal life, manners, and
theology,—evidencing a knowledge of earth
and sky, of providence and grace, and a command of thought, sentiment, language, and
literary power, which no mere man has ever
equalled. In it we find a familiarity with
writing, engraving in stone, mining, metallurgy,
building, shipping, natural history, astronomy,
and science in general, showing an advanced,
organized, and exalted state of society, answering exactly to what pertains above all to the
sons of Joktan, whose descendants spread
themselves from Upper Arabia to the South
Seas, and from the Persian Gulf to the pillars
of Hercules, tracking their course as the first
teachers of our modern world with the greatest
monuments that antiquity contains.

THE PRIMITIVE CIVILIZERS.

It has become the fashion to refer all this
to Arabian Cushites, or a people of Hamitic
blood, but it is one of the blunders of the
would-be wise. Because the name of Cush,
usually rendered Ethiopia, became early at-
tached to some undefined portions of Arabia,
and because the children of Canaan originally
settled in Palestine, therefore everything relat-

ing to prehistoric Arabians and dwellers
along the Mediterranean shores must needs be
credited to the children of Ham, though it
should leave to the Shemites scarce a place on
earth! Such a theory may have its day, but
there is every evidence, biblical and secular,
literary and monumental, that the greatest
and mightiest population of the ancient Arabia
was mainly, if not exclusively, of pre-Abrahamic Shemitic stock. The tribes which possessed it were mostly of the seed of Joktan,
son of Eber, till the descendants of Abraham
through Esau and Keturah, and the descendants of Lot, began to fill in from the north-
west.* These Joktanites were the true Arabians, and the superior people who occupied
the most important portions of the country,
populated its shores, gave it their Heberic language, cultivated every interest of human
society and greatness, planted their colonies in
Eastern Africa, around the whole eastern coast

---

* "Ethnologers are now agreed," says Rawlinson, "that in
Arabia there have been three distinct phases of colonization—
first, the Cushite occupation, recorded in Gen. 10 : 7 ; secondly,
the settlement of the Joktanites, described in verses 26–30 of
the same chapter ; and thirdly, the entrance of the Ishmaelites,
which must have been nearly synchronous with the establishment of the Jews in Palestine."—Rawlinson's *Herodotus*, vol.
i, p. 357.

of the Mediterranean, and westward as far as
Carthage, the Guadalquiver, and the shores of
the Atlantic. They were

> The true ancient Erythræan stock,
> E'en that sage race who first essayed the deep,
> And wafted merchandise to courts unknown;

> The first great founders of the world,
> Of cities, and of mighty states, and who first viewed
> The starry lights, and formed them into schemes.*

---

* The names of the progenitors of these peoples, and the
notices we have of them and their descendants, abundantly indicate all this.

Almodad means *the measurer*, and the Chaldee paraphrase of
Onkelos and Jonathan attests that he was accounted the inventor of geometry, and the man who lined or measured the
earth with lines; hence, also a great astronomer.

Of *Sheleph*, the same paraphrase says that he led forth the
waters of rivers, that is, instituted canals, and operated in
water-works, perhaps the inventor of water-mills.

Hazarmaveth gave his name to a country which still bears it,
and was, according to tradition, a great grammarian.

Jerah, the fourth son of Joktan, who is called *Ierab* in the
ancient Arabic records and traditions, is the man from whom
we have the name of *Arabia*, the land of Ierab. He gave his
name to a province of Tehama, in which he settled, and thence
it became extended to the country in general, which the natives
still call the Peninsula of Ierab; son of Joktan, whom the
Arabians call Kahtan. The Jerachæans were growers of
grains, miners, and refiners of gold.

Uzal peopled the great country of Yemen, "famous from
all antiquity for the happiness of its climate, its fertility, and
riches." Its capital, *Sanaa*—the city of *learning*—vied with
Damascus in the abundance of its fruits, and the pleasantness
of its water. His descendants were manufacturers, merchants,
and travelling traders, whom Ezekiel refers to as present in the
fairs of Tyre, with possessions of bright iron, cassia, and
calamus.

Nor does it argue anything against Job's
being Joktan's son, that in the Mosaic or sub-

Dikla was the father of a great tribe of traffickers in aro-
matics.

Obal peopled the southern extremity of Arabia, whence
colonies crossed the Straits of Babelmandeb, and took possession of the bay still called after him, the *Avalitic*. His descendants were great merchants, and carried on large trade in the
best myrrh, and other odorous drugs, also in ivory, tortoise-
shell, tin, wheat, and wine.

Sheba was the father of one of the tribes of the Sabeans.
There was a tribe of Cushite-Sabeans, whose vulgar depreda-
tions are referred to in the Book of Job, and also a later tribe
headed by a son of Jokshan, grandson of Abraham The Joktanic Sabeans were located near the Red Sea, and were the
richest of all the ancient Arabians in gold, silver, and precious
stones.   Ezekiel mentions them as trading with ancient Tyre.
They were metallurgists, lapidaries, and dealers in all rare lux-
uries.   They were among the wisest and most intelligent, as
well as the richest and most enterprising of ancient peoples.
It was their queen who came to hear the wisdom of Solomon,
and from among them, according to the Egyptian accounts, there
came up delegations to visit and view the Great Pyramid as if
comprehending and reverencing it as no Egyptians ever did.

Ophir is the very word for wealth, and from the name of the
descendants of this son of Joktan, we have our word *magazine*,
illustrative of their consequence as bankers and depositaries of
treasures.   From them Solomon got almug trees for pillars to
the temple, brought in the ships of Hiram, himself being of this
same Joktanic blood and language

And with *Job* to complete the list we have here beyond
question the most illustrious family of peoples of prehistoric
times.

Baldwin, in his *Prehistoric Nations*, says, " It would be unreasonable to deny or doubt that in ages farther back in the
past than the beginnings of any old nation mentioned in our

sequent editing of the Book of Job, his friends
are said to be from countries called after the

ancient histories, Arabia was the seat of a great and influen-
tial civilization.   This fact, so clearly indicated in the remains
of antiquity, seems indispensable to a satisfactory solution of
many problems that arise in the course of linguistic and archæological inquiry.   It is now admitted that they were the first
civilizers and builders throughout Western Asia, and they are
traced by remains of their language, their architecture, and the
influence of their civilization on both shores of the Mediterranean.   It is apparent that no other race did so much to develop
and spread civilization, that no other people had such an extended and successful system of colonization, that they seem to
have monopolized the agencies and activities of commerce by
sea and land, and that they were the lordly and ruling race of
their time.   The Arabians were the great maritime people of
the world in ages beyond the reach of tradition.   As Phœnicians
and Southern Arabians they controlled the seas in later times,
and they were still the chief navigators and traders on the
Indian Ocean when Vasquez di Gama went to India around the
Cape of Good Hope."—Pp. 66, 67.

From Herodotus we learn that the Phœnicians came from the
Erythræan Sea, which he explains to be the Persian Gulf, that
having crossed over from thence they established themselves on
the coast of Syria on the Mediterranean, and that their chief
cities were Tyre and Sidon.   McCausland says they were once
supreme throughout the Mediterranean, and even beyond the
pillars of Hercules.   Tyre sent forth numerous colonies and
founded flourishing commercial communities in various parts
of the world.   Her merchant princes spread their dominion
over Cyprus and Crete and the smaller islands of the Archi-
pelago in their vicinity.   They also made settlements in Sardinia,
Sicily, and Spain, and their vessels penetrated as far as the
islands of Madeira to the west, and to the British Isles and the
Baltic on the north.   Traces also are found of them in India,
Ceylon, and onward across the Pacific to the shores of the New
World.   Carthage, for a long time the rival of the Roman

names of some of Abraham's descendants.
Names which did not exist for thousands of

Aryans, was the most flourishing and last surviving of the
Phœnician colonies. The renowned Hamilcar and Hannibal
were members of this family, also Cadmus, who was the first
to introduce letters into Greece, and Ninus, the just and wise
king of Crete, who according to Thucydides, was the first
known founder of a maritime empire.—McCausland's *Builders
of Babel*, pp. 53–55.

That the Phœnicians were Shemitic, and not Hamites, is
proven by their language, which from the inscriptions they
have left is manifestly and incontrovertibly the same for the
most part and in every case with what is familiar to the
modern student as *Hebrew.* See Gesenius's *Scripturæ Linguæque
Phœniciæ Monumenta,* where that distinguished scholar, as Gale
and others have also observed, says "Omnino hoc tenendum
est, pleraque et pæne omnia cum Hebræis convenire, sive radices
spectas, sive verborum et formandorum et flectendorum ra-
tionem."

Rawlinson, in his *Essays* on Herodotus, Bunsen, in his *Philosophy of Un. History,* and Wilkins, in his *Phœnicia and
Israel,* with every degree of confidence assert and maintain
that the Phœnicians were *Shemites,* and hence of the Joktanic
lineage. Rawlinson also remarks that these people possessed
"a wonderful capacity for affecting the spiritual condition of
our species, by projecting into the fermenting mass of human
thought new and strange ideas, especially those of the most
abstract kind. Shemitic races have influenced far more than
any others the history of the world's mental progress, and the
principal intellectual revolutions which have taken place are
traceable in the main to them."—*Herodotus,* p. 539.

An item of evidence of Melchisedec's connection with this
people is found in the name of the Deity given in Gen. 14 : 18,
where the God of Melchisedec is called, not *Eloah* or *Elohim,*
but *Eliun,* which is the Phœnician designation of God used by
Sanchoniathon, the Phœnician sage, from whom sundry fragments have been preserved. See Kenrick's *Phœnicia,* p. 288.

years afterwards are in like manner given to
the country about the Garden of Eden. (Gen.
2 : 11–14.)

There is no evidence that the chief river of
Palestine bore the name *Jordan—River of
Dan*—till long after the time of Moses and
Joshua, and yet that subsequent Jewish name
is everywhere inserted in the antecedent records.   And so Eliphaz might much more intelligibly be said in Moses' time to have been
from the country then known as Teman, and
Bildad from the country then known as Shuah,
though they both lived and occupied those
regions hundreds of years before Teman and
Shuah were born.   There may also have been
an earlier Teman and Shuah whose names
others long after them in some way inherited.
The original name of the territory in general
is preserved in the designation of the country
of Job himself, which also plainly antedates
the Teman and Shuah descended from Abraham.   From Stony Arabia to Damascus, along
the whole east of Palestine, the country is
called *Uz*.   The more precise region whence
Job came, likely was that portion of Arabia
bordering on the east of Edom, south of Trach-
onitis, and extending indefinitely towards the
Euphrates.   *Uz* is a Shemitic name, called

Aws in the Arabian antiquities, and denotes the region where Shem himself probably lived and died.* Judging from chapter 8 : 8–10, and 12 : 12, we may readily believe that Job himself saw, heard, and often consulted Shem, and got his sacred wisdom from him. In the providence of God he in a measure at least, and perhaps by special call and ordination, took Shem's place as the principal representative of the patriarchal religion after Shem's death, as Abraham subsequently, whom Melchisedec blessed and consecrated as meant to fill this office after him, till he, of whom Melchisedec was the illustrious type, should come.†

JOB AND PHILITIS.

And as Melchisedec and Job were most likely one and the same person, so the same would seem to be the *Philition* of Great Pyramid notoriety. Job was the youngest of a

---

* "Shem appears in his own annals as one who had left his native [original] land, and in the course of ages migrated west and south from the primitive common seat of the civilized stock of Central Asia, with an unceasing tendency towards Egypt."—BUNSEN'S *Univ. Hist.*

† This would give us a most remarkable and unbroken succession or line of sacred prophets from the foundation of the world—Adam, Seth, Enoch, Noah, Shem, Job, Abraham and the chosen people, terminating in Jesus Christ and his Church, which abides to the end of this present world.

family in which was the science, faith, and enterprise for such a work, beyond all others then living.   Job was an Arabian, and a shepherd prince, just as the Egyptian fragments testify respecting Philitis.   Job's account of his own greatness, doings, and successes, depicted with so much beauty in chapter 29, grandly harmonizes with Manetho's story of the strange power of the Hicsos over the Egyptian rulers obtained " without a battle." He held idolatry to be a crime punishable by the authorities (chap. 31 : 26–28), just as Cheops was persuaded while the Great Pyramid was building.   He was a true man of God, a public instructor in sacred things, with whom Jehovah communicated, and whom the Spirit of God inspired.*   The Almighty speaks to

---

* Dr. Lee renders chap. 29 : 7, " When I went forth from the gate *to the pulpit* and prepared my seat in the broad place " Herder translates the same,

" When from my house I went to the assembly,
    And spread my carpet in the place of meeting."

In verses 21–23, there is a further allusion to his addresses to the people, and the reverence and eagerness with which they listened to him.

The account of the convening of " the sons of God," given in the first chapter, implies the existence of assemblies for worship in those times, and the giving forth of instruction on those occasions.

him in chapter 38 as if he were the identical person who had laid the measures of the Great Pyramid, stretched the lines upon it, set its foundations in their sockets, and laid its topstone amid songs of exalted triumph.* Chap. 19 : 23–27 looks like a description of the high intent of the Great Pyramid, and a prayer that it might endure with its glorious freight even to the end of the world. And the more I study the Book of Job in the light of its author's identity with the mysterious Arabian stranger to whom the Egyptians attribute the Great Pyramid, the stronger and

---

* The spirit of the passage admirably interprets in this sense. The object is to convince Job of his incompetency to judge of and understand God, and the address runs as if the Almighty intended to say to him, " *You* laid the foundations of the great structure in Egypt, but where were you when I laid the foundations of the far greater pyramid of the earth ? *You* laid the measures on the pyramid in Egypt, but who laid the measures of the earth, and stretched the line upon it ? *You* fastened down in sockets the foundations of the pyramid in Egypt, but whereupon are the foundations of the earth fastened ? *You* laid the pyramid's completing capstone amid songs and jubilations, but who laid the capstone of the earth when the celestial morning stars sang together, and all the heavenly sons of God shouted for joy ?" The image is unquestionably that of the pyramid, and the appeal is best interpreted and tenfold intensified on the hypothesis that it was the builder of that pyramid who is thus addressed. This would also give adequate reason for the departure from the idea of the earth's nature and position given in another part of the book, to take up the image of a pyramidal edifice in this grand passage.

more satisfying to me becomes the likelihood
that here is the mighty prince and preacher
of Jehovah from whom we have that monument. All the facts, dates, and circumstances
amply accord with the theory that "Melchisedec" was Job, and that the same was the
"Philition" of Herodotus.

But whether such identity can be established or not, the effect in this argument is
essentially the same. If these three names
denote three distinct persons, they all belong
to the time of the Great Pyramid's erection
and to the same general community or class
of people. They were all shepherd princes.
They all hated idolatry, worshipped the true
God, and fulfilled a sacred mission mostly
before Abraham came upon the stage. And
closely related to them were others of the
same faith and spirit, and scarcely inferior in
dignity. Eliphaz, and Bildad, and Zophar,
and Elihu, must be counted with them, and
of them we may judge from what we read and
hear of them from the Book of Job. From
all these together we get an impression of the
age and communities in which they had their
homes, and what sort of men then lived and
operated. What we find in them we may put

down as characteristic of their period, and from it safely reason.

RESULTS.

We thus learn what is indeed of very great moment, to wit, that God then had his priests and worshippers upon earth, and that they were the most princely, learned, and commanding people living. We thus learn that it was God's habit to converse with them, to direct their ways by special revelations, and to inspire them for the utterance and recording of his mind, will, and purposes. We thus learn that they were the family kindred and blood relatives, the same in language and country, with those whence the after world obtained all the original elements of science and civilization. We thus learn that with them was the competency and every qualification, both natural and supernatural, for the erection of just such a monument of science, theology, and prophetic history, as we find in the Great Pyramid. Nay more, we thus learn that it was the subject of their special craving, that their words, wisdom, and immortal hopes should be engraven with pens of iron in imperishable memorials of rock! (Job 19 : 23–27.)

No matter then whether Philitis, Melchisedec and Job were one, or two, or three; such mighty men of Jehovah there were in that far-off age. They believed in one God, and in holy angels, and in a devil, whose subtle depravity had inoculated all natural humanity. They feared sin, and sought forgiveness and salvation through bloody sacrifice. They hoped for a coming Redeemer, and for resurrection through him. They treasured the primeval records, traditions, and revelations from Adam down, even the same from which Moses compiled when he framed his Genesis.*

* From Luke 1 : 69, 70, and Acts 3 : 21, we learn that there were sacred prophets, inspired of God, from the earliest beginnings of human history. Who were they? Adam, Seth, Enoch, Noah, and Shem were most eminent among the primeval worthies, and most blessed and honored of God of all the ancients; these would then be the greatest sacred teachers, and the men most fitted to hand down accounts of the things they saw and had learned of the Lord. The indications also are that they did severally record and transmit what they knew and held as sacred, and that Moses in making up the Book of Genesis incorporated these sacred heirlooms into his records, weaving them into one narrative, condensing, adding to, but carefully preserving the ancient texts which he employed. Hence the name of the art called *Mosaic work.* Nor would it seem impossible, even at this late day, to point out what parts of the holy records have come from each.

I. If we take Genesis 2 : 4, on to the end of the third chapter as the *Book of the Prophet Adam*, it at once assumes a life and vividness which it does not otherwise possess. Its title and contents show that it is a monograph. Its close would seem to

Special communications, teachings and impulses from God were also as common to these people

indicate the time when it was written and its probable author. Certainly no one was so well qualified to write it as Adam himself. And if he wrote anything, it must above all have been this. Assuming also that he, and not Moses, was the original narrator, we are greatly helped with regard to the allusions to the topography of Eden, which doubtless was much changed, at least in the apprehensions with which men looked upon the geography of the earth in the time of Moses, from what it was in the time of Adam. Two thousand years make a wonderful difference in the statements of a gazetteer, even with regard to the same localities. The account of the temptation and fall also becomes more intelligible and interesting in its simplicity as Adam's own statement, than as that of so remote a historian as Moses. The name for the Deity (*Jehovah Elohim*), *Jehovah God*, is also peculiar to this one section of the divine word.

II. Genesis 4: 1-26 is again a distinct monograph, the close seeming to indicate the author, who speaks of the Deity always under the name *Jehovah*. If we have anything from Seth, this is the section above all others that would fall to him. It is perhaps only the conclusion of an ampler record from that holy patriarch.

III. From Enoch we certainly have at least a fragment which is preserved in the Epistle of Jude, beginning at verse 14. He uses the name of Deity the same as Seth.

IV. From Noah we would seem to have several books, the first including Gen. 5: 1-32. Its title shows its monographic character, and its close indicates when and by whom it was written. It denotes the Deity exclusively by the one name (*Elohim*) *God*.

V. A second Book of Noah would seem to be Gen. 4: 9-22; 7: 7-24; 8: 1-19; 9: 1-27. None was so competent to write this account as he, and the occurrences are so wonderful that it could hardly be otherwise than that he would, as a preacher of righteousness, have solemnly recorded this momentous account. Its end is indicated by a change in the name denoting the

as to Abraham after them.   (See Job 4 : 12, 13;
6 : 10 ; 23 : 12 ; 33 : 14–16 ; 38 : 1 ; 42 : 5–7.)

Deity in what follows.   It also adds greatly to the life character of the narrative to take it as from the hand of him who
was the most deeply concerned in the matter.

VI. There is probably a third Book of Noah, in the form of
an apocalypse of the creation work, given in Gen. 1 : 1–31;
2 : 1–3. The nature of this revelation was quite apart from
any personal experience or recollection, and could as well have
been given to one prophet as another. The form of designating
the Deity (*Elohim*) is that in the sections which appear to have
come from Noah, and the style corresponds to those sections as
to no other portions of the Bible. It is a complete monograph
in itself, and can be best conceived by referring it to the
prophet Noah.

VII. Genesis 4 : 1–4, 6–8 ; 7 : 1–6; 8 : 20–22; 9 : 28, 29; 11 :
1–9, shows quite a different style from either of the other sections. It does not appear as a continuation of the Noachian
narrative, but rather as fragments of an independent account,
from which Moses has interwoven parts to give a greater fulness to the record in general. It designates the Deity (*Jehovah*)
the same as Seth and Enoch, and not as either Adam or Noah.
The author evidently lived after Noah, though personally
familiar with the affairs attending and following the deluge.
Therefore, it is most probable that we have these fragments
from the patriarch Shem.

VIII. So, Genesis 10 : 1–32 and Genesis 11 : 10–26, are plainly
monographs, and as plainly from distinct sources. Had Moses
been the original author of both, the one would have been
made to correspond with the other, and we would have had one
symmetrical statement of the genealogy, continuous and di-
gested. The first bears internal evidence, amounting almost
to certainty, that it was composed by Eber from his own personal knowledge, and while living with his younger son
Joktan. That it was written before Sodom was destroyed is
proven by verse 19. Had it been written by Moses, he
would not have said, " *as thou goest unto Sodom and Gomorrah,*

They had the moral and intellectual qualifications to furnish the sublimest section of the holy Scriptures. There was no superior enlightenment, no higher civilization, no purer faith, no truer science, no more intimate famil-

---

and Admah and Zeboim," but *" as thou goest unto the Salt Sea,"* as in Deut. 3 : 17 and elsewhere. The genealogy in the eleventh chapter is also more orderly in style, and was most likely made up by Terah or Abraham, from information handed down from father to son in the family from which he was himself descended.

It would be presumption to speak confidently on such a subject, or to claim that this is beyond mistake the authorship of these several sections of the sacred word. The inspiration of Moses is warrant enough for all of them. But Moses nowhere claims to have been the original author of these records, neither does the Scripture assert that they were written by him. On the contrary, it tells us of a succession of inspired men from Adam's time, from whom we have nothing, except as above indicated. And as the nearer the historian lived to the events which he relates, the more satisfactory his account ; if there is reason to believe that these documents were written by the parties personally concerned, they become the more impressive, interesting, and easy to be understood.

It is at least interesting to take the Bible and read the several portions as above assigned to Adam, Seth, Enoch, Noah, Shem, etc., in order to see what life and spirit these records take on, when viewed in a way which is at once so probable and so fully in accord with other statements of the Scriptures.

From the texts in Luke and Acts it is clear that the Gospel is as old as the race, and that there never was a time when it was unknown and unsounded. It is traceable in the constellations of the heavens, as represented of old ; it is reflected in the traditions and mythologies of all ancient peoples, and in every age there were holy prophets who treasured the divine oracles, and prophesied and taught concerning the coming and achievements of Jesus Christ, and " the restitution of all things."

iarity with the works and purposes of God, than they possessed. And a princely member of their mysterious and loving brotherhood it was who dwelt in Egypt while the Great Pyramid was building. Having obtained peaceable possession of the king's heart, he induced him to shut the temples, punish the priests, cast out the gods, and lend his royal co-operation for the building of a pillar to Jehovah of hosts, which should last to the end of time, and which men should open and read in this last evil age, and know that it is from Him who is about to judge the world for its apostasies.

Thus then, by a chain of traditions, facts, and Bible testimonies, we connect the origin of the Great Pyramid with a mighty prehistoric people, wholly separate from Egypt and its abominations,—a people among whom inspiration, as true and high as that of Moses, wrought, and from whom we have not only the noblest of the sacred books, but likewise the noblest edifice on earth, equally fraught with holy intelligence, divine truth, and inspired prophecy.

What have we then in this unrivalled pillar, but A MIRACLE IN STONE—a petrifaction of wisdom and truth, revealed of God, preserved among his people from the foundation of the world, and thus memorialized by impulse and aid from Him, that it might outlive the apostasies of man, and stand as a witness to the Lord Almighty when he cometh to judge the world, and to fulfil his promise of " the restitution of all things."

Men may combat and scorn a conclusion so sublime. They may utterly reject it, as they also rejected Christ, and still reject his salvation. But it involves nothing impossible—nothing improbable—nothing but what we might reasonably expect in view of what God did in ancient times, and promised to the fathers. It is agreeable to every item of history of which we can avail ourselves. It conforms to the remarkable traditions on the subject, which cannot otherwise be accounted for. Passages and allusions in both Testaments imply, if they do not positively declare, that it is a thing of God. And the great monument itself gives palpable demonstration of what cannot be rationally explained on any other hypothesis.

PRIMEVAL MAN.

Materialistic and skeptical science appears disposed to settle upon the belief that man is a being who has had to educate himself up to

what he is, from a troglodyte, if not from something much lower. Of course this goes against
the Scriptures, and sets aside as fable and
mythic superstition all the most essential substance of the Scriptures. But what care such
scientists for that? Such consequences to a
theory they take rather as a recommendation.
But no such philosophizing can stand before
the Great Pyramid. If the primeval man was
nothing but a gorilla or a troglodyte, how, in
those far prehistoric times, could the builders
of this mighty structure have known what
our profoundest *savants*, after a score of centuries of observation and experiment, have
been able to find out only imperfectly? How
could they know even to make and handle the
tools, machines, and expedients indispensable
to the construction of an edifice so enormous
in dimensions, so massive in its materials, so
exalted in its height, and so perfect in its
workmanship, that to this day it is without a
rival on earth? How could they know the
spherity, rotation, diameter, density, latitudes,
poles, land distribution, and temperature of
the earth, or its astronomic relations? How
could they solve the problem of the squaring
of the circle, calculate the π proportion, or determine the four cardinal points? How could

they frame charts of history and dispensations, true to fact in every particular for the space of four thousand years after their time, and down even to the final consummations ? How could they know when the Mosaic economy would start, how long continue, and in what eventuate ? How could they know when Christianity would be introduced, by what great facts and features it would be marked, and what would be the characteristics, career, and end of the Church of Christ ?   How could they know of the grand precessional cycle, the length of its duration, the number of days in the true year, the mean distance of the sun from the earth, and the exact positions of the stars at the time the Great Pyramid was built? How could they devise a standard and system of measures and weights, so evenly fitted to each other, so beneficently conformed to the common wants of man, and so perfectly harmonized with all the facts of nature ?   And how could they know to put all these things on record in one single piece of masonry, without one verbal or pictorial inscription, yet proof against all the ravages and changes of time, and capable of being read and understood down to the very end of the world ?

Yet, THESE THINGS THEY DID KNOW !   Here

they are in solid stone, displayed to all eyes, and challenging the scrutiny of all the *savants* of the earth. Men may sneer, but they cannot laugh down this mighty structure, nor scoff out of it the angles, proportions, measures, nature references, and sacred correspondences which its makers gave it. Here they are in all their speaking significance, stubborn and invincible beyond all power to suppress them. Nothing now can blot out this record, and on it is written the true Scriptural dignity of primeval man, fashioned in the image of his Maker, furnished of God with everything requisite to his highest life on earth, and illumined and impelled of heaven to make this memorial of his sacred possessions, ere they should be finally lost amid the ever-increasing deterioration. It is a record whose antiquity none can dispute, whose authenticity none could corrupt, and whose readings none can construe without the admission of a Divine intervention!

And then what? Why *then inspiration is a demonstrated reality,—then miracle is a tangible fact,—then the foundations of infidelity are dissolved,—then the Scriptures are true,—*AND THEN OUR CHRISTIAN FAITH AND HOPES ARE SURE, AND CANNOT DISAPPOINT US!

Wondrous Providence of a wondrous God, to have planted in our world such a memorial as this,—

> Building in stone a real revelation,
> Which in Time's fulness has at last been read!

USE OF THE PYRAMID RESPECTING FAITH.

It is not a substitute for our glorious Bible that we find in this marvellous pillar, nor a thing to be put on equality with the Scriptures, as though the written word were in any manner deficient. We throw back the imputation that we would propound a new religion with a new oracle. Our vaulting scientists have quite monopolized that business. The world resounds with the pratings of their varied sects and schools, agreeing in nothing but in negations of the supernatural. We are content with what our holy books record. But when a sacrilegious rationalism would emasculate them, and an Epicurean philosophy would trample them into the slough, we rejoice and thank God that before he gave these books he caused this mighty pillar to be stationed in the very path of vaunting science, that his assailed, abused, and oft-bewildered children in the extremity of the ages might be able to appeal to it exultantly for monumental attestation of their faith, and, amid the wrinkles and infirmities of failing Time, still have to show an unfaded memorial of its glorious youth.

GLORY BE TO THE FATHER, AND TO THE SON, AND TO THE HOLY GHOST; AS IT WAS IN THE BEGINNING, IS NOW, AND EVER SHALL BE, WORLD WITHOUT END. AMEN.

APPENDIX.

EXTRACTS FROM RECENT WRITERS.

As a sequel to the preceding lectures, it may be proper, and may give satisfaction to many readers, to present the opinions and statements of some others, in their own words, with regard to this interesting subject. A few such extracts are accordingly inserted here by way of *appendix*.

REV. JOSEPH TAYLOR GOODSIR, F.R.S.E.

" I believe that several important things fully warrant us in maintaining that there was, when the Great Pyramid was builded, and that there is now, a very sufficient final cause for the rearing of such a scientific symbol as it has the best claim to be considered. The urgency of this final cause may be seen to have been great at first, because in spite of all that had occurred at Babel, the two chief nations of earliest antiquity, Chaldea and Egypt, had determinedly adopted sabaism as their worship, either by itself or mixed with other superstitions ; and secondly, it is great in these times when a lamentable number doubt or avowedly disbelieve, and even laugh at, that Biblical record to which the world owes its present freedom from sabaism and innumerable other evils, and when many would ask us to take Lucretius as our Bible, and a Lucretius, too, expurgated even of the pagan's allusion to a remote region in which he allowed there might be gods, but gods who cared not for man or his affairs.

" At the earlier of the two periods referred to, the Great Pyramid, possessing the character proven to belong to it,

(233)

would act as a standard protest against sabaism and other idolatries, and also against the injustice which invariably asserts predominance over the mass of mankind, when they enlist themselves in the service of falsehood.　Certain scientific and physical conditions required that the magnificent protesting fabric should be placed in Egypt rather than in Babylonia, the seat of the undivided sway of sabaïsm. But there is no reason to believe that intercourse between the primeval nations was so limited that the religious and moral lessons intended to be taught by the chief wonder of the world at that time could not reach from Egypt to Babylon.　Doubtless it would be treated by the followers of sabaism in Babylon just as it appears to have been by those in Egypt.　That is to say, there would be continuance in sabaism in Babylon just as there was in Egypt after the strong hands of the royal builder, who trod under his feet Egyptian gods, were powerless in death.　At the same time the Egyptians would appear to have retained and handed down a partial knowledge of the true character of the pyramid, until it became gradually obscured, and was at last quite lost.　But amongst the worshippers of the Lord God the knowledge of its true character was long preserved, as would appear from the symbolic use of it made in the Book of Job, and elsewhere in Scripture.　The traditional knowledge of it, or of the science symbolized by it, preserved among the people of God, was one means we believe of saving them from that worship of the sun, moon, and stars which Job declared to deserve, even on its first appearance, death at the hands of the magistrate.　And I may state that for my own part I trace the fountain of physical knowledge which was opened by God for primeval man, and which was symbolized by the Great Pyramid, certain approaches made by some Greek philosophers to some cosmical views deemed to belong purely to modern times.　These philosophers themselves ascribe their knowledge of these things to Eastern and Egyptian sources. Thus, Thales held all things to have originated in a fluid substance ; Lucippus, the earliest Greek teacher of the atomic theory, held, as Aristotle tells us Pythagoras did, that the heavenly bodies revolve about each other, committing the error indeed of making the sun revolve about the moon, but still teaching truly that the earth revolves about the sun, and also about its own axis, by which last the alternation of day and night is caused. It appears to me that what is true in this early astronomical view is so far removed from the obvious and common conception of the subject, as to warrant the idea that the erroneous portion of the statement was man's corruption of the pure primeval knowledge symbolized by the Great Pyramid, for this among other reasons, that it might show us in these last days how God supplied physical knowledge to primeval man that he might be warned against such monstrous superstitions as sabaism, and that the possession of a measure of such knowledge might preserve his true worshippers from many destructive errors.

" But again, this primeval monument, after the lapse of more than four millenniums since its construction, is subserving at this very day most important purposes as respects wisdom and knowledge. The gradual disclosure of its scientific mysteries is a result in a great measure of the partial dilapidation it has suffered, especially during the times of the barbarous Mohammedan rule. The number and importance of the lessons which its disclosed mystery teaches is indeed very striking. Thus it testifies to the state of the stellar heavens at the time of its building, and teaches at the same time its own age. It helps also to determine the date of the flood, and to give consistency to the chronology and history of diluvian and post-diluvian times. It testifies to the importance of the exact and of the physical sciences—terrestrial and cosmical—not merely from the utilitarian, but from the religious point of view. It shows that some unidolatrous men possessed extraordinary knowledge in these sciences just when the whole world was going widely astray in the worship of sun, moon and stars, and it thus seals, as with a divine impress left on adamantine materials, the truth that sound science is not only a handmaid but a defender of sound religion. Moreover, it shows the symbols of just weights builded into a most durable repertory, as they were afterwards laid up in the temple of Jerusalem, at the very time when a brutal tyranny was gradually overspreading the idolatrous world, which may be said to have had its chief seats in Egypt, and in Babel, the capitol of Nimrod, that mighty hunter before the Lord—a tyranny which, instead of revering a justice determined scientifically according to the measures and weights employed by Opifex Mundi himself when he 'fetched a compass round the universe,' and 'weighed the hills in a balance,' despised all justice, and crushed the body of mankind down into beasts of burden.

"Such are the things taught us at this day by the Great Pyramid, as there are noble men of science sufficiently animated with Christian truthfulness and courage manfully to proclaim. We thus see a united science, righteousness, and religion testifying from the Great Pyramid with a reawakened mien, just as they were intended to do more than four thousand years ago. The oldest and noblest building is thus seen to be at one in testimony and in spirit with the oldest and noblest book. God is making that great name for himself, I believe, by the Great Pyramid at this day, which the builders of the tower of Babel sought to make for themselves. If there be any truth in the opinion of those who believe that they can point to some of the remains of the tower of Babel, then these now present only a mass of rubbish, blasted and vitrified by the wrathful fires of heaven, though the chief part of the buildings has undoubtedly sunk out of human sight into the soft alluvial soil on which they were so unwisely erected. Their only lesson is that of desolation wrought by a just divine vengeance, and the shortcomings of human ideas. The Great Pyramid, on the other hand, is lasting as the hills, even as the rocky hill on which it is so securely founded, while the very denudations it has experienced by the torrents of barbarism rather than of the elements, have only furthered God's plan of making it his witness to scientific truth in its relations with justice and religion in these last days.

"Putting together then the various things we have insisted on, I ask whether it is after all so wild and chimerical an idea that God should have stirred up, in the primeval age of the world, men who knew him, and who inherited or had imparted to them a divinely taught science to construct this greatest of all builded monuments ? Is not this rather the *rational* view to take of it ? Here, for one thing, is a scientific symbol, as measurements, calculations, and reasonings of an incontrovertible kind prove it to be. This matter stands on its own basis. Again, Scripture contains a number of allusions and symbolic expressions which find no object so exactly and completely suitable as this confessed ' wonder ' of the ancient world. This also stands on its own basis. Still further, some such sufficient reason as the symbolism of the Great Pyramid presents is required to account for the wise and sensible views of the Cosmos entertained by the true worshippers of God from the earliest ages. This is certainly a consideration of weight not easily cast aside. In this last consideration is also seen one part of the final cause for the construction of a symbol like the Great Pyramid shortly after the arrangement of the building of the tower of Babel, while another portion of this final cause is seen in the inestimable benefits, historical, economic, moral, and religious, conferred on us by the scientific character of the Great Pyramid at this day.

" Here, then, are four firmly grounded, quite independent reasons, which unite in supporting the beautiful and no less valuable theory as to the divine authorship of the Great Pyramid. We can discern clearly in our subject also the illustration and confirmation of this grand moral truth : Man's ambitions and wicked designs for making a name to himself, as a power without God, are invariably blasted and end in shame, but God's works endure and testify to the glory of that name which will outlast the sun, moon, and stars."—*Seven Homilies on Ethnic Inspiration*, 1871, pp. 59–64.

J. RALSTON SKINNER.

" To a mind unbiassed by the prepossession of a theory, the assertion that the Great Pyramid of Egypt was built to perpetuate a series of measures, astronomical and otherwise, and to contain a mathematical and geometrical system of calculation and admeasurement, cannot be received with incredulity. . . .

" As to the objects of its construction, one may be taken as *astronomical*, for the facts that the north base side coincides with the parallel of 30° north latitude, and that the mass, as to its sides, evidenced by its corner socket lines, is oriented as perfectly as could be expected of human ability. Another may be taken as *geometrical*, as it was so built that its height should be to one-half its circumference as diameter to circumference of a circle. . . .

" Hence it exhibits itself as one not only monumenting a method of quadrature, the elements of which we possess, but also a measure of the sun's time, and also the inch and foot values. . . .

" This measure is just that one that, with the ancients, seems to have stamped the whole system as natural or divine, *i.e.*, showing that man was but dealing in measures in some sort shadowing forth mechanical principles of construction, which it had pleased the Creator of all things to adopt as the law of creation.

" The original (ideal) pyramid, whence the real pyramid of the Nile springs, is directly constructed from the original elements of relation of diameter to circumference of a circle. This is circular elements *one*. On the lines of this original pyramid springs another, whose elements are circle *two*. Out of the elements *two* another set of elements is obtainable, governing the interior work of the pyramid proper; these elements are those of circle *three.* (Problems given in detail.)

"These are the circles whence the complete pyramid, as to its outside and as to its inside, is fitly framed and put together, giving the measures of the heavens and the earth.

"While the triangle represents the pyramid, the triangle and circle represent the elements from which the plane measure of the square of the base of the pyramid is derived. . . .

"The author believes it to be shown that the elements of construction of the pyramid, and their use, agreeably to the intention of the architect, have been proved, and that these are shown to be used as the foundation of the Bible structure from the first chapter of Genesis to the closing scenes of the New Testament.

"But while these elements are rational and scientific, and in the Bible rationally and scientifically used, let no man consider that with this discovery comes a cutting off of the *spirituality* of the Bible intention, or of man's relation to this spiritual foundation. No house was ever actually built with tangible material until first the architectural design of building had been accomplished, no matter whether the structure was palace or hovel. So with these elements and numbers. They are not of man, nor are they of his invention. They have been revealed to him to the extent of his ability to realize a system which is the creative system of the eternal God, open at all times to man for his advance into its knowledge, just in the measure of his application and brain ability, free to all as is the water we drink and the air we breathe. But spiritually to man the value of this matter is, that he can actually in contemplation bridge over all material construction of the Cosmos, and pass into the very thought and mind of God, to the extent of recognizing this system of design for cosmic creation—yea, even before the words went forth, *Let there be!* It is the realization of the existence and mental workings of the Divine Mind, by means of the little primal cube and its circle, which to us are tangible realities, and goes to prove to man that his soul lives, and will continue to live, and thus he may take little heed for his body, which is, however exquisitely constructed, but a mask dulling the finer power of his mental whole.

" The best and most authentic vehicle of communication from God to man, though many exist, is to be found in the Hebrew Bible, the preservation of which in its exactitudes can only be ascribed to a spiritual supervision. A like preservation of a real monument of the practical application of the Bible secret stands to-day on the banks of the Nile."—*Key to the Hebrew-Egyptian Mystery in the Source of Measures*, 1875.

CHARLES CASEY, Esq.

"It is unnecessary to multiply Eastern authority for the sacred and scientific character of the Pyramid as opposing and superior to the Western belief in the tombic theory, which, however, naturally arose and was confirmed by the erroneous conclusion that the use and character of the primary pyramid might be truly predicated from the unquestionable tombic pyramids of a later date. It strikes the writer that as far as argument goes touching the features claimed for the building, it would make no difference whatever if a massive mural tablet had been found set in the masonry of the exterior, a lid found on the Coffer, a mummy of Cheops in it, etc., etc., as the fact would still remain, that the mausoleum (if you will) and sarcophagus (if so insisted) were designed by an architect who embodied in their construction all the primary truths claimed and verified, while still leaving them suited to secondary and inferior uses, just as the Royal *Scytale* of the Spartan kings, while essential to translating a decree on which hung the fate of nations, might serve to be used for any secondary purpose.

" Therefore, the real and only question is, Whether the

Great Pyramid does or does not contain the metric features claimed for it ? If it does, there remains no doubt that the architect who embodied the truths exhibited must have been superhumanly inspired, as in the age in which he lived no such knowledge existed among men [except from Revelation]. If it does not contain those metric features, demonstrative refutation is within reach of line and rule, and the Pyramid stands to be questioned of and reply for itself to all gainsayers.

" To those who reply, ' We admit the measures, but we deny the conclusions drawn from them,' the answer is, that if the measures, as in the instance of the base side length giving the length of the solar tropical year, exhibited but one instance of preconceived design, it might be said that such coincidence was accidental, but when a concatenated chain of design is shown of the highest order of scientific knowledge, the denial of such design in the mind of the architect is of that class which refutes itself by the absurdity of its assertion.

" Every dispassionate reader who has paid due attention to the argument advanced must be impressed with the conviction that in this our day and generation, no more important question or discovery has arisen or been made than the character and revelation of this Sethic monument, the Great Pyramid, in, but not of, Egypt."—*Philitis, or the Solution of the Mystery,* 1876, pp. 36, 37.

JOHN TAYLOR

" When so many evidences of the scientific knowledge of the founders of the Great Pyramid present themselves, these facts cannot be disregarded. The difficulty may be great in supposing a people to have been in existence at that early period, who were capable of executing a work of so vast a magnitude on purely scientific principles, but is it not also probable, that to some individuals God may have given the knowledge, even at that early age of the world, for which we are now contending ? How could Noah have built the

ark if he had not been divinely instructed as to its fabrica-
tion ? And might he not have been equally instructed in
the knowledge requisite to form the Great Pyramid ? Both
these wonderful works are based on *measure*, and the latter
structure shows a knowledge of those measures which were
in use before the flood, as well as of those which were afterwards established, implying therefore an acquaintance with
antediluvian things. How could the Arabian numerals,
and the knowledge by which they were so arranged as to
increase tenfold in power by change of position, have been
discovered so soon after the deluge, if the same system had
not existed before, or if divine assistance had not been
granted at so early a period after that event ? Even after
these figures had once been known, the majority of mankind for at least three thousand years remained ignorant of
their use, and never again hit upon the arrangement as a
discovery.

"Moses, we are told, was *admonished of God* when he
was about to make the Tabernacle, which was to serve as
the example and shadow of heavenly things, ' for see, saith
he, that thou make all things according to the pattern
shewed to thee in the Mount.' There is an orginality in
the character of these early revelations, which shows them
to have had a higher source than that of man's present intelligence, great as it may seem. Our modern discoveries
are rather *inferential*, consisting chiefly in the application
to things known to purposes previously unknown. Of this
kind is the invention of the art of printing. I would not
detract from the importance of modern discoveries, but I
think they seem to benefit mankind less than the communication of the art of ship-building, of the Arabian system
of enumeration, of geometry, or the means of measuring
the earth, and of the art of alphabetic writing :

'So thoughts beyond their thoughts to those high bards were given.'

" In regard to the Great Pyramid, it was the happy discovery of the two casing stones, when all were thought to

be destroyed, which at once changed conjecture into certainty. We now probably know all that we shall ever know respecting the origin and purpose of the Great Pyramid, and all that we require to know. We now find that all the seemingly different measures, when properly understood, are equal to each other, and mean the same thing. By the knowledge derived from the angle of the casing stones, and the length of the base of the Great Pyramid, all those measures of proportion which seem arbitrary in the *Table of Constants*, are found to be no longer so. The measures of the earth are no less certainly established.

" When we find in so complicated a series of figures as that which the measures of the Great Pyramid and of the earth require for their expression, round numbers present themselves, or such as leave no remainder, we may be sure we have arrived at primitive measures."—*The Great Pyramid, Why was it Built? and Who Built It?* 1864.

PIAZZI SMYTH, F.R.S.E., F.R.A.S.

ASTRONOMER ROYAL FOR SCOTLAND.

" What then is, or is to be, the end or use for which the Great Pyramid was built ?

" The *manner* of that end appears—on putting facts together—to have been, to subserve in the fifth thousand of years of its existence certain preordained intentions of God's will in the government of this world of man.

" I presume not to speak to any other than such parts of the building as have already practically developed themselves. Herein, too, enough seems now to have shone forth to enable any one to state roundly that the message wherefor the Great Pyramid was built is largely of a duplicate character, or thus :

" (A) To convey a new proof to men in the present age as to the existence of the personal God of Scripture, and of his actual supranatural interferences in patriarchal times with the physical and otherwise only natural experi-

ence of men upon earth.   Or to prove in spite, and yet by
means, of modern science, which in too many cases denies
miracles, the actual occurrence of an ancient miracle, and
if of one, the possibility of all miracles recorded in the
Scriptures.

"(B) In fulfilment of the first prophecy of Genesis, which
teaches, together with all the prophets, that of the seed of
the woman without the man, a truly Divine Saviour of
mankind was to arise and appear amongst men, in poverty,
too, and humility ; in further fulfilment thereof, the Great
Pyramid was to prove that precisely as that coming was a
real historical event, and took place at a definite and long-
preordained date, so his second coming, when he shall de-
scend as the Lord from heaven, with the view of reigning
over all mankind, and ruling them all with one divine
sceptre, and under one all-just, beneficent, omnipotent
sway, that that great event will likewise be historical, and
will take place at a definite and also a primevally pre-
arranged date.

"Now let us look a little closer into the first of these.

"It would seem to be, that an omniscient mind which
foresaw in the beginning the whole history of the world
under man (especially the widespread science knowledge of
our day), ordained that the message, arguments, proofs of
the Great Pyramid should not be expressed in letters of any
written language whatever, whether living or dead, but in
terms of scientific facts, or features amenable to nothing
but science, *i. e.*, a medium for the communication of ideas
to be humanly known and interpretable only in the latter
day.

"Not in the day of the Great Pyramid at all, but rather
since the revival of learning in Europe, no pure mathematical question has taken such extensive hold on the human
mind as ' the squaring of the circle.'   Quite right that it
should be so, for a time at least, seeing that it is the basis
alike of practical mathematics or high astronomy.   That
quantity under the form of π proportion, given in almost

every text-book of mathematics to more decimal places than there is any practical occasion for, having been ascertained for one hundred or more years, men might rest content and go on to other subjects. But numbers of them do not and will not. Hardly a year passes but some new squarer of the circle appears, generally a self-educated man. But occasionally the most highly educated university mathematicians also enter the field, and bring out perchance some new algebraic series by which a more rapid conveyance to the true numbers of π may be obtained. That numerical expression is shown on all hands and in all countries to be one of the most wonderful lasting characteristics and necessary results of the growth of science for all kinds and degrees of intellectual man, and in an increasing proportion as they arrive at a high state of civilization, material progress, and practical development.

" Is it not then a little strange that the first aspect which catches the eye of a scientific man looking with science and power at the ancient Great Pyramid, is that its entire mass in its every separate particle, all goes to make up one grand and particular mathematical figure expressing the true value of π ? If this was accident, it was a very rare accident, for none of the other thirty-seven known pyramids of Egypt contain it. But it was not accident in the Great Pyramid, for the minuter details of its interior, as shown, signally confirm the grand outlines of the exterior, and show again and again those peculiar proportions, both for line and area, which emphatically make the Great Pyramid to be, as to shape, a π-shaped and a π-memorializing pyramid,—the earliest demonstration known of the numerical value of that particular form of squaring the circle which men are still trying their hands and heads upon.

" Again, in physics, as a further scientific advance on the foundations of pure mathematics, is there any question so replete with interest to all human kind as what supports the earth, when as Job truly remarked, it is hung from nothing, suspended over empty space, and yet does not fall? As it regularly revolves around a bright central orb, and in such a manner as to obtain therefrom light and heat suitable to man, and day and night, what is the nature of that path which it so describes, and what is the distance of the physical life luminary round which it now revolves ? As in squaring the circle, so in measuring the distance of the earth's central sun, both learned and unlearned have been working at the question for twenty-three hundred years, and are still employing themselves upon it. Nothing that nations can do is thought too much to devote to this question of questions in physics for the future behoof of a world grown scientific. Yet *there* is the numerical expression for that cosmical quantity nailed to the mast of the Great Pyramid from the earliest ages, for it is its mast or vertical height multiplied by its own factor, the ninth power of ten, which is the length all modern men are seeking, and struggling, and dying in order to get a tolerably close approach to the arithmetical figure of. And this accurate sun distance at the Pyramid is accompanied by an exhibition of the space travelled over during a whole circle of the earth's revolution, and the time in which it is performed.

"And if from solar system quantities we turn to matters of our own planet world in itself alone,—does not every inhabitant thereof yearn to known its size, and yet was not that impossible to all men of all the early ages to attain with any exactness ? But precisely that thing which all mankind from the creation up to the day of Job had not accomplished, and had no idea or power how to set about to perform it, and did not make even any rude attempts in that direction during the following twenty-five hundred years—though they do know it now with tolerable accuracy—was not only well known to the author of the design of the Great Pyramid, but was there employed as that most useful standard in terms of which the base side length is laid out, or with accurate decimal reference to the earth's peculiar figure, its polar compression, the amount thereof, and the most perfect method of preserving the record for all men. Who but the Lord could have done that wonder above man's power *then* to do ? Who, indeed, but the God of Israel could have performed this last-mentioned still greater wonder than any mere linear measure, so far as its exceeding difficulty to men even in the present scientific generation is concerned, and could have actually introduced into the King's Chamber Coffer, and the said chamber itself, an expression for the next most important quality after size, of the earthball we live upon—viz., its 'mean density,' besides expressing in the base diagonals of the Pyramid the enormous cycle of years composing the earth's disturbed rotation or precession period of the equinoxes ?

" Yet, with all this amount of science brought before us out of the Great Pyramid, yea, even with all this quintessence of scientific results, let us not be run away with by the notion of some, that to teach science was the beginning and end for which that building was erected. . . .

" The second part of the end wherefor the Great Pyramid was built, I have already said, appears to begin somewhat thus, viz., to show the reality and the settled as well as long preordained times and seasons for each of the two comings of Christ,—both for that one which has been (eighteen hundred and seventy-seven years ago), under whose then commenced spiritual dispensation we are still living, and also for that other one in kingly glory and power which is yet to beam upon us.

" *When* that second coming has been appointed to take place must be a most momentous question, and it is one to which I can only reply, that so far as the Great Pyramid seems to indicate at present in the Grand Gallery, the existing Christian dispensation must first close in some manner or degree, the saints be removed, and a period of trouble and darkness commence, for how long it is difficult to say, seeing that the scale of a pyramid inch to a year appears to change there. Very long the time can hardly be, if the pyramid standards of the metrology of that universal kingdom, the only successful universal kingdom that there ever will be on earth, the kingdom of the Lord Christ, are already beginning to appear from out of the place of security where they were deposited in the beginning of the world."—*Our Inheritance in the Great Pyramid*, 1874, pp. 463–479.

J. G., IN EDINBURGH EVENING COURANT, MAY 9th, 1868.

" In our opinion the idea of a Divine interposition in the planning and construction of the Great Pyramid, when closely contemplated as springing from all the facts and relations of the case, is perfectly rational and credible in the estimation of a rightly instructed mind. Rightly instructed mind, we say, for a man may be mighty in ' midden ' philosophy, and ignorant as a child in that great mother science of catholic and revealed theology, based on the grand design argument uttered by the Cosmos, on the wide testimony of universal history and tradition, and on that testimony of human nature to religion which is so inextinguishable that it drives the very atheistic positivists into that ineffably sad idolatry of humanity itself. It is on this grand testimony that the astronomer royal for Scotland builds, and we rejoice to be of one mind with him. And this, not because we think the truth of religion, as the grandest historical element, is dependent on the truth of the theory as to the Great Pyramid, but because the principles involved in the full argumentation of this theory are among the principles of catholic theology according to our description of it, and accordingly, whether the case of the Great Pyramid be one to which these principles are rightly applied or not, the principles themselves dare not be pooh-poohed. The self-called ' advanced thinkers ' of the archæological schools may scout them, but we hold, on the universal testimony of sacred and profane history, that man's story does not take its rise in a dunghill. Our creed in this matter is that blessed belief handed down in Scripture, and chanted by

the grand choir of historians and poets. The theory of the
Pyramid, too, falls in completely with the grand strain. It
points, on the ground of remarkable facts and coincidences,
to the Great Pyramid as an instance of those divine interpositions which are known on the testimony of Scripture,
corroborated by tradition, to have been made as occasion
called for them, during the infant ages of the world.

"Moreover, the Great Pyramid, viewed in the light of
this theory, is seen to be a peculiar one among other elements of prophecy, cast by Divine Providence as seed on
the waters among the nations, to ripen in due time and
serve most beneficent ends in the appointed season.

"There existed in the religious books of the ancient Persians, undoubted prophetic and apocalyptic elements, which
certainly contributed along with other elements in the
Magian system to form that character which fitted Cyrus
and his Persians to punish the grossly idolatrous Babylon-
ians, and free God's ancient people. Again, if ever there
was a clear case of divine interposition of the more ordinary kind employed for great moral and religious ends, it
may be seen in the moral and religious revival, such as it
was, that took its rise in pagan Greece in the person of Soc-
rates, and all that sprang from the influence, example,
and teaching cast into society by that noble martyr.
Still again, it is a matter of notoriety that the Romans
treasured in the Capitol certain Sibylline books, that can be
shown *not* to have been favorable to polytheism, still less to
pantheism, and that they not only fell in remarkably in
certain prophetic statements with the Hebrew Scriptures,
but influenced the conduct of leading Romans themselves.
All these we devoutly believe to have been arranged and
provided by God, even as we know from history that they
formed powerful elements in forces that moved the cardinal
events in human history. And is any one so blind as not
to see that we live in times as momentous as any since those
of the flood, excepting those years when the Lord of Glory
himself dwelt upon earth ? For how many are ready to

shout Io Pæan ! in the vain hope that at last the 'vile superstition,' as they call it, taught in the holy Scriptures, and so marvellously supported, is doomed to a speedy extinction ?   Others are busily helping on this sure consummation, as they believe it, by advancing and fostering a strange philosophy, which (whatever lip worship some of its sects may pay to revelation, yet in reality) takes man up at first as an ape-descended animal, reared in barbarism, and destined in the end (so far as their philosophy can show) only to make manure for the soil he sprang from.

" When forced to hearken to such degrading opinions, is it not a boon to be thankful for, when there is presented to our contemplation a most noble builded work, which proves how far removed from savageism its architects were, at a period when history and tradition alike testify that man and the world had just emerged from an awful catastrophe ? For in saying this we stand well supported, and defy any one to disprove on the only valid and allowable ground— that of universal history and catholic theology—the reasonableness and credibility of God's interfering to instruct and guide an architect, who knew and worshipped him, in the rearing of a grand symbolic building, suited according to divine foreknowledge, at least to stagger, and suggest wiser views to, certain of the 'advanced thinkers,' and rather too pensive *a priori* philosophers, of these latter days."—Reprinted in *Antiquity of Intellectual Man*, 1868, pp. 476-485.